THE TRANSFORMATION OF
AGRICULTURE IN THE WEST

NEW PERSPECTIVES ON THE PAST

General Editor
R. I. Moore

Advisory Editors
Gerald Aylmer, Tanya Luhrmann, David Turley, Patrick Wormald

This series is designed to examine the broad issues and questions which are constantly touched upon in historical study, but are rarely examined directly. From a basis of sound and specific historical scholarship the authors explore their chosen themes, ranging widely across cultures and long periods of time, and often using the concepts and interpretations of other disciplines.

PUBLISHED

David Arnold   Famine
James Casey   The History of the Family
Patricia Crone   Pre-Industrial Societies
Ernest Gellner   Nations and Nationalism
David Grigg   The Transformation of Agriculture in the West
Richard Hodges   Primitive and Peasant Markets
Eugene Kamenka   Bureaucracy
Edward Peters   Torture
Jonathan Powis   Aristocracy

IN PREPARATION

David Arnold   Culture and Environment
Richard Bonney   Absolutism
Bernard Crick   Representative Institutions
Ernest Gellner   Reason and Culture
David Gress   The Modern State
R. M. Hartwell   Capitalism
John MacKenzie   Hunting
Linda Levy Peck   Patronage
David Turley   Slavery
James Fentress and Chris Wickham   Social Memory

THE TRANSFORMATION OF AGRICULTURE IN THE WEST

David Grigg

BLACKWELL
Oxford UK & Cambridge USA

First published 1992

Basil Blackwell Ltd
108 Cowley Road, Oxford, OX4 1JF, UK

Basil Blackwell, Inc.
3 Cambridge Center
Cambridge, Massachusetts 02142, USA

Library of Congress Cataloging in Publication Data
A CIP catalog record for this book is available from the Library of Congress.

British Library Cataloguing in Publication Data
A CIP catalogue record for this book is available from the British
Library.

ISBN 0-631-17093-6
ISBN 0-631-17094-4 Pbk

Typeset in 10 on 12 pt Plantin
by Graphicraft Typesetters Ltd, Hong Kong
Printed in Great Britain by Billing & Sons Ltd, Worcester

This book is printed on acid-free paper.

For Jill, Susan, Catherine and Stephen
with much love

Contents

Editor's Preface

Ignorance has many forms, and all of them are dangerous. In the nineteenth and twentieth centuries our chief effort has been to free ourselves from tradition and superstition in large questions, and from the error in small ones upon which they rest, by redefining the fields of knowledge and evolving in each the distinctive method appropriate for its cultivation. The achievement has been incalculable, but not without cost. As each new subject has developed a specialist vocabulary to permit rapid and precise reference to its own common and rapidly growing stock of ideas and discoveries, and come to require a greater depth of expertise from its specialists, scholars have been cut off by their own erudition not only from mankind at large, but from the findings of workers in other fields, and even in other parts of their own. Isolation diminishes not only the usefulness but the soundness of their labours when energies are exclusively devoted to eliminating the small blemishes so embarrassingly obvious to the fellow-professional on the next patch, instead of avoiding others that may loom much larger from, as it were, a more distant vantage point. Marc Bloch observed a contradiction in the attitudes of many historians: 'when it is a question of ascertaining whether or not some human act has really taken place, they cannot be too painstaking. If they proceed to the reasons for that act, they are content with the merest appearance, ordinarily founded upon one of those maxims of common-place psychology which are neither more nor less true than their opposites.' When the historian peeps across the fence he sees his neighbours, in literature, perhaps, or sociology, just as complacent in relying on historical platitudes which are naive, simplistic or obsolete.

New Perspectives on the Past represents not a reaction against specialization, which would be a romantic absurdity, but an attempt to come to terms with it. The authors, of course, are specialists, and their thought and conclusions rest on the foundation of distinguished professional research in different periods and fields. Here they will free themselves, as far as it is possible, from the constraints of subject, region and period within which they ordinarily and necessarily work, to discuss problems simply as problems, and not as 'history' or 'politics' or 'economics'. They will write for specialists, because we are all specialists now, and for laymen, because we are all laymen.

The discovery of agriculture around ten thousand years ago made possible the concentrations of human population without which there could have been no history. Its development secured the surpluses which maintained minorities of specialists in craft, prayer and government, fuelling the rise and fall of civilizations. But it also created a thraldom which still grips much of the world. Once humanity's numbers were allowed to exceed what could be supported by the intricate balance between the hunter-gatherer and his environment they could be sustained only by an incessant struggle for food. The year-round, day-in day-out demands of crops and cattle, even more than the hopeless vulnerability of settled populations to extortion and taxation, condemned most cultivators to a precarious, poverty-stricken and unremitting toil from which, as the fearful human girdles of so many of the world's cities still bear witness, many of them have been determined to escape at almost any price.

The 'agricultural revolution' of the last few centuries has therefore been much more than the prelude of the 'industrial revolution' to which we glibly attribute the making of the modern world. The great transformation which David Grigg describes is first of all a transformation in the ways and conditions in which food has been produced, but its implications are staggering. For most of human history perhaps nineteen people in twenty laboured on the land; two hundred years ago it was still three out of four in the most advanced regions; now it is one in twenty. Bringing this about, as Grigg shows, involved far more than technical progress in agriculture itself, essential though that was. Its results touch every facet of human life on earth, for better and for worse. Nobody who hopes to understand the present or to anticipate the future dare overlook it.

R. I. Moore

Figures

Tables

Acknowledgements

I am very grateful to Mrs Joan Dunn and Mrs Margaret Gray for their rapid and efficient typing of this book and to Graham Allsop and Paul Coles, who drew the figures with their characteristic care and dispatch. Bob Moore not only suggested I write the book, but made many important suggestions about the structure of the text, corrected errors and smoothed my rough-hewn prose. To all, I give my thanks.

1
Introduction

In the last two centuries there have been great changes in the material life of the western world – the countries of Western Europe, North America and Australasia. First has been the remarkable increase in their population; from only 25 million in AD 1000 it rose to 110 million in 1800 (including 6 million in North America), and to 650 million in 1985. In other words, the population quadrupled in 800 years, but then rose nearly sixfold in the next 180 years. Second has been a great change in the way in which people earn their living. In the eighteenth century 70 per cent or more of the population worked in agriculture; this has now fallen to less than 5 per cent, and the great majority of the population earn their living in mining, manufacturing or, and of increasing importance in the last thirty years, services of various kinds. This change in occupation has led to a change in where people live: 200 years ago three-quarters of the population lived in isolated farmhouses, hamlets, villages or small country towns; now, in spite of the decline of inner cities and the growth of commuter villages, the great majority of the population is urban. A further change has taken place in the speed and cost of travel, both for people and for goods.

These changes have been accompanied by, indeed most would say caused, an increase in the wealth of nations and a rise in the standard of living of the majority of the people of these countries. In 1800 most of the population lived in what modern writers would call absolute poverty; now a minority live in relative poverty. These developments are immediately visible in improved housing, holidays, and the array of consumer durables, from motorcars to microwave ovens, owned by modern Europeans. More fundamentally, expectation of life at birth has risen from forty years or less to over seventy, and malnutrition and famine have been virtually banished. Modern men and women are taller, fitter, healthier and stronger than their forebears.

There is a large literature on these changes; indeed, understanding how they have come about is a central concern of many economists, historians, sociologists and geographers. Some have focused upon the changes in social life – the change from traditional *mores* to modern; others, the majority, upon the nature and reasons for economic development: the great changes in occupational structure; and economic growth – the rise in income *per capita* of nations and individuals. Whatever the approach, the centre of discussion has invariably been industrialization and urbanization. Agricultural change has been neglected, for in modernization it is the agricultural economy of traditional society that has been replaced. Yet farming has undergone remarkable changes over the last two centuries, and it merits attention, even if it has been a declining part of all economies going through the process of economic development and modernization; for without the modernization of agriculture, economic growth could not have been sustained. This book tries to demonstrate the major changes that have occurred in the farming of North America, Western Europe and Australasia since the eighteenth century – and in some cases over a much longer period, for the processes that have brought about the modernization of agriculture have worked themselves out over a very long period.

The nature of change

Modern farming shows a great many differences from the traditional agriculture of the early modern period, in the crops grown, the livestock raised, the sources of power, the implements and machinery used and in the scale and organization of production. But the two fundamental differences are, first, the capacity of modern agriculture to increase output at a very high rate, and second, the much higher productivity of land and labour.

Before the nineteenth century the agricultural output of Western Europe increased only very slowly, but increase it did, for the population was about 60 million in 1300 but 105 million in 1800, a rate of population increase of 0.11 per cent per annum over the 500 years. As the consumption of food per head was not a great deal higher in 1800 than in 1300, agricultural output probably did not increase at much above the rate of population growth. Most historians believe that the rate of increase of output quickened from the seventeenth century, at least in England. But E. L. Jones has suggested that output increased no more than between 25 and 57 per cent in the sixteenth century, 25–36 per cent in the seventeenth century, and even in the eighteenth century, which most historians believe saw the beginnings of modern agriculture, only 61 per cent. Other experts put the rate of agricultural growth in eighteenth-century England at 0.6–0.7 per cent per annum, in France at only 0.5 per cent per annum.

Since then the output of most agricultural economies in the West has increased at prodigious rates. German farm output tripled in the nineteenth century, in France it increased ninefold between 1700 and 1960, and in England by the same proportion between 1800 and 1980; whilst the output of United States agriculture in the 1940s was seventeen times what it was in 1800. These rates of increase slackened in the early twentieth century, but have grown very rapidly since the 1930s. French agricultural output doubled over the nineteenth century; but it increased by two-thirds between 1959 and 1977 alone. In most western countries output has at least doubled in the last half-century.

Productivity growth

Agricultural output can be increased simply by increasing the area sown to crops, or the number of livestock kept, or by the number of hours worked. But increases in these factors, or in the capital used in agriculture, do not account for the great leaps in output achieved in the last two centuries. Since the eighteenth century there have been great increases in agricultural productivity.

Agricultural productivity is conventionally measured in two ways. The first is by output per hectare, or land productivity. This can be raised either by increasing crop yields or by shifting from a system of farming which produces a relatively low value of output per hectare – such as sheep grazing – to an intensive system that produces a high value per hectare, such as horticulture. Second, productivity can be measured by relating total output to the number of people working in agriculture – labour productivity. Increases in labour productivity can be obtained in a number of ways, but the most important has been through replacing the labour of men, animals and simple implements with power-driven machines.

This has given great increases in output per man, particularly over the last thirty years. However, there are rarely adequate statistics to measure the hours worked or the value of total output over long periods; an alternative measure is the number of hours needed to complete specific agricultural tasks at different dates.

Productivity increases since 1800

There is much disagreement about the trend in crop yields before the nineteenth century, for there are few comprehensive statistics. Some believe there was little change over very long periods before 1800. But after 1800 increases in yields were dramatic in most parts of Western Europe, although less so in North America or Australasia until after the 1930s. The increase of wheat yields in France is indicative of the long-term trend in crop yields (figure 1.1).

Output per man is more difficult to trace; one estimate suggests that in French agriculture it is now five times what it was in the eighteenth century. But much larger long-term increases have occured. English agricultural output is now about nine times what it was in 1800, but the labour force is no more than a quarter what of it was in that period, suggesting a far greater increase of labour productivity in the transition from traditional to modern agriculture. The introduction of machinery has led to dramatic declines in the amount of labour needed to produce crops. Thus in the 1950s the production of wheat in the United States needed only 7 per cent of the labour required in 1800 (figure 1.1).

Traditional agriculture

This book is concerned with the transformation of traditional farming, as practised in Western Europe and North America before the early nineteenth century. Thereafter, industrialization profoundly affected agriculture and the process of agricultural modernization. Nevertheless, traditional agriculture was not static. Indeed, the agricultural revolution that many historians have described in the late seventeenth and eighteenth centuries took place *before* industrialization and before modernization took place. Before the 1820s and 1830s there were increases in output and productivity, but these were dwarfed by what followed.

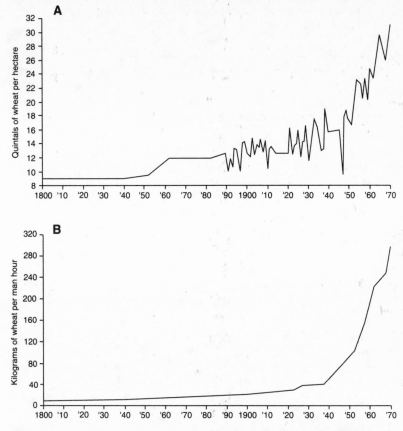

Figure 1.1   The growth of productivity in modern agriculture, 1800–
1970. (A) Quintals of wheat per hectare in France; (B) kilograms of wheat
per man-hour in the USA, 1800–1970. (*Source*: P. Hohenburg, 'Maize in
French agriculture', *Journal of European Economic History*, 6, 1977, 63–102; United
States Department of Commerce, *Historical Statistics of the United States*, *Colonial
Times to 1970*, Washington DC, 1975.)

Traditional agriculture had a number of characteristics (table
1.1). In most of Europe where it was pursued, 75 per cent or more
of the population were engaged in agriculture and few lived in
towns. Consequently most of the product was consumed on the
farms themselves, and the size of the market was limited. Without
refrigeration perishable products could not be moved far, and the
high cost of transport prevented much long-distance movement of
foodstuffs except by sea. Productivity in farming was low; average

Table 1.1 Characteristics of traditional and modern agriculture

	Traditional	Modern
Percentage of produce sold off farm	Less than 50%	More than 50%
Percentage of inputs purchased	Less than 10%	More than 30%
Percentage of workforce in agriculture	More than 70%	Less than 10%
Crop yields	1000–2000 kg per hectare	4000 kg and over per hectare
Source of fertilizers	Animals, residues, waste, legumes, bones etc.	Chemical fertilizers
Weed and pest control	Rotations, inter-cropping, fallowing, biological control	Herbicides and pesticides
Labour inputs per hectare	High	Low
Land *per capita* of workforce	Low	High
Source of power	Human and animal muscle	Tractors and electricity
Degree of specialization	Low	High
Leading inputs	Land and labour	Capital

wheat yields rarely exceeded 1340 kg bushels per hectare before the nineteenth century, compared with about 5000 kg today, and were generally lower. Most of the inputs that farmers used in production were available on the farm. Livestock produced manure, implements were simple and made locally, weeds were controlled by cultivation, and pests and disease by rotations and biological control. The seed used came from the preceding harvest, often one-quarter or more of the total. Power came from human and animal muscle. Most farmers tried to produce as much as possible of their food and other needs, so that few specialized in one crop or livestock type. Indeed, nearly all farmers combined crop production and livestock production. As long as transport costs were high, specialization was difficult, and took place mainly near large towns or rivers, where transport costs were lower; and comparatively few farmers sold most of their produce off the farm.

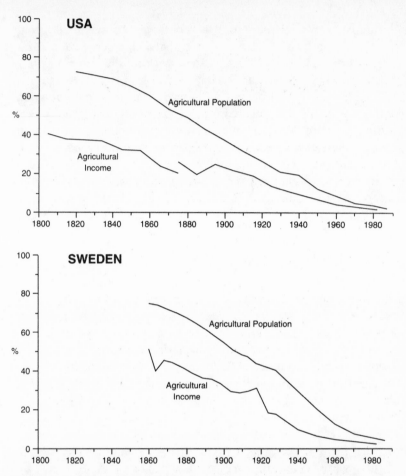

Figure 1.2 The decline of agricultural income and agricultural population as a proportion of total national income and total working population, USA and Sweden. (*Source*: E. M. Ojala, *Agriculture and Economic Progress*, London, 1952, pp. 27, 44, 50, 85.)

Industrialization

Industrialization brought profound changes to agriculture in Europe and North America; paradoxically the most rapid change in farming has come as agriculture has declined both as a proportion of the workforce and in its contribution to the value of output (figure 1.2). Until the later eighteenth century farming was the occupation of over 70 per cent of the population in every country in

Europe, with the exception of Britain and the Low Countries, but with industrialization the numbers employed in manufacturing, mining, transport and later in services, steadily increased and increased more rapidly than the number working on farms.

As industrialization got under way it had important effects upon agriculture. First was the rapid growth of demand; population growth and urbanization increased the size of the farmer's market as more and more of the population had to purchase their food. In the later nineteenth century growing prosperity increased demand for more expensive products such as meat, milk, fruit and fresh vegetables, and so changed the structure of output.

Second, farmers began to buy an increasing proportion of their inputs from off the farm, from the industrial sector. This began with the development of an agricultural machinery industry. Until the eighteenth century most implements were made locally, mainly from wood, except for the cutting edges. With the growth of an iron industry, firms specializing in agricultural implements produced large numbers of machines. From the 1840s the use of animal manure was supplemented by chemical fertilizers, although it was not until the 1920s that nitrogen fertilizers could be produced cheaply and the use of fertilizer dramatically increased. In the eighteenth and nineteenth centuries, seed merchants were established, although they were not fully effective until advances were made in plant breeding in the early twentieth century. Nor did this exhaust the services and inputs bought from off the farm: tiles for underdrainage, and specialized services such as those of veterinary surgeons and accountants, grew in importance; animal feedstuffs were, from the early nineteenth century, made up by compounders rather than on the farm; whilst power came in the nineteenth century from coal, later in the twentieth century from petroleum and national grid electricity. Thus the modernization of agriculture has seen a distinct rise in the proportion of inputs purchased off the farm. In the case of Sweden, for example, such purchases were insignificant in the mid-nineteenth century, then rose steadily and dramatically after the end of the Second World War (figure 1.3). By the 1960s purchased inputs accounted for at least half of the value of gross output in most western countries.

Agriculture was also affected indirectly by industrialization, especially in two important ways. In the later nineteenth century the attraction of jobs in towns – which had long existed – became

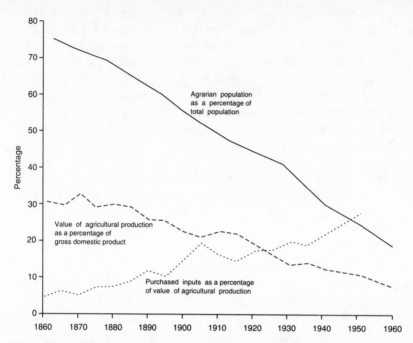

Figure 1.3 Purchased inputs as a percentage of the gross value of
agricultural production, Sweden, 1860–1950. (*Source*: A. Simantov, 'The
dynamics of growth and agriculture', *Zeitschrift fur Nationalökonomie*, 27, 1967, pp.
328–51.)

so great that agricultural populations ceased to increase, and eventually decreased as out-migration to the towns exceeded natural
increase, thus prompting the need for mechanization. In Europe
this decline began in the British Isles in the 1850s, but by the
beginning of the twentieth century agricultural populations were
stagnant in most of Western Europe, although the great decline in
numbers began only after 1945. From the 1850s the spread of
railways and the introduction of refrigeration lowered the cost of
transporting agricultural produce. On an international scale it ex-
posed Western Europe to competition from the low-cost producers
of North America and Australasia. Both forces accelerated the
specialization of agricultural production; farmers ceased to grow a
wide range of products and concentrated upon a few commodities,
whilst cheaper transport allowed areas to specialize in particular
products.

Lastly, whilst industrialization has allowed farmers to substitute inputs made by industry for local and farm-produced products, much of the processing of raw materials once done on the farm – such as butter – and cheesemaking – is now done in factories, whilst an increasing proportion of all farm produce is processed in some way. Indeed, in some parts of the food production system, food processers have taken control of production on the farm.

The aim of this book is to describe the way in which output and productivity increased both in traditional agriculture, before the impact of industrialization, and during modernization, in the period since industrialization. But the emphasis is laid more on the nineteenth and twentieth centuries than is done in most accounts of agricultural change, because the pace of change – whether measured by the increase in output or productivity – is so much greater since industrialization than before. It may be, as many historians have argued, that an industrial revolution could not have taken place without a preceding agricultural revolution; it is certainly true that the effect of the industrial revolution upon agriculture has been remarkable.

2
Land

There are two ways in which agricultural output can be increased. The area used for cultivation can be expanded, more crops grown and more livestock raised upon it. Alternatively more can be produced from land already in cultivation. This in turn can be done in two ways. The yield of crops – the output per hectare – can be increased by using more fertilizer or by more frequent and careful cultivation. Or the land can be used differently, by changing to a system of farming which permits a higher output per hectare. Thus, for example, much of the American Mid-West was used for ranching in the early nineteenth century; later the land was used for growing maize and feeding it to pigs. Increasing yields and increasing the area in cultivation are not mutually exclusive. In the early nineteenth century the agricultural output of much of Western Europe was increased both by reclamation of swamp and woodland and by increasing crop yields.

However, the relative importance of increasing output by these two means has changed fundamentally. In traditional agriculture most of the increases in output came from increasing the area cultivated; during the modernization of agriculture, and particularly in the twentieth century, most of the extra output has come from increases in the output per hectare. This is a result of changes in the relative importance of the factors of production. In traditional agriculture, land and labour were the two most important inputs; in modern agriculture labour inputs have declined dramatically, land has shown little change, and capital – fertilizers, feedstuffs, machinery and pesticides – has increased. This change has occurred only in this century, as the United States exemplifies (table 2.1).

Increasing the area in cultivation

Before 1840 there was no reliable census of agriculture in any country in Western Europe. Yet there is no doubt that the area

Table 2.1   The changing relative importance of labour, capital and land, USA (percentage of total input in US agriculture)

	Work	Land	Capital
1910	75.0	8.0	17.0
1960	30.0	9.0	61.0

Source: J. N. Lewis, 'The changing importance of land as a factor of production in farming', *Proceedings of the Twelfth International Conference of Agricultural Economics, Lyon, France*, London, 1966, pp. 420–38.

then in cultivation greatly exceeded that of the Middle Ages. But even when statistics are available, there are problems in interpreting changes in land use, because of the considerable variations both in the way in which land can be used and in the ways in which its use is recorded. Land defined as arable includes all land used regularly for crops, comprising not only annual crops such as wheat or turnips, but permanent crops such as olives or apples. In addition those grasses grown in rotation with cereals and other crops are included in this category. But the major problem is that in both national censuses and earlier estimates of land use by contemporaries land in bare fallow is counted as part of the arable area. Before the nineteenth century a large proportion of arable was in fallow in any one year; so the arable area is not a good guide to the area sown with crops.

The term 'pasture' has always been used in agricultural censuses and in less formal estimates of land use to describe land used for grazing livestock. Unfortunately, what is meant by pasture varies from country to country and at different times in the past. Thus in Britain two types of grazing land are recorded in census statistics: permanent grass and rough grazing. The latter consists mainly of semi-natural vegetation such as heather, bilberries, scrub and poor grass, and is grazed at a low intensity. Much of the Scottish Highlands, the Pennines and upland Wales is recorded in the agricultural census as rough grazing. Permanent grass is enclosed, sown with good grass varieties and may receive fertilizer. In contrast, in German national statistics no distinction is made between permanent grassland and rough grazing, and so care must be taken when comparing the two countries. But this problem is even greater when comparing countries in Western Europe with those in North America and Australia, where very large areas of semi-arid land, with a much lower productivity than land in Western Europe, are recorded as permanent pasture. Thus the account of expansion given here is of the *arable area*.

The expansion of the arable area in Western Europe

Although Western Europe's arable area in 1800 was well above what it had been in the Middle Ages, the expansion of the area in cultivation has not been continuous, but has chiefly taken place when the price of cereals has risen rapidly, and more rapidly than the price of livestock products; this has encouraged farmers to reclaim land and increase the area in crops. In periods of stable or falling cereal prices, in contrast, the area in cultivation has been constant or declined, and livestock production has assumed a greater relative importance. These different price periods correspond to periods of change in population.

The eleventh, twelfth and thirteenth centuries were a period of comparatively rapid economic growth. In AD 900 much of Europe was covered by forest, but the following centuries saw the removal of woodland to allow cultivation (figures 2.1 and 2.2). Between AD 1000 and 1300 much of the lowland forest was removed in Central and Western Europe, and cultivation also extended into mountain areas, notably in the Vosges, Alps and Pyrenees. In England settlements were found on Dartmoor and the North Yorkshire Moors at altitudes higher than at any subsequent period. In the lowlands the loam soils were much prized because of their ease of cultivation; heavy clay soils were, on the other hand, shunned, and many – such as those in the Sologne, south of Paris – were not cultivated until the nineteenth century.

Coastal areas saw much reclamation, and embankments were built to protect low-lying land both from the sea and from estuarine flooding in Lincolnshire and Norfolk, on the Elbe, the Loire, the coast of Flanders, and most notably in the Zuider Zee. Less spectacular was the steady encroachment of each village into the surrounding forest, reclaiming fields one by one as population mounted. More dramatic was the expansion of Western Europe's agricultural frontier. In the north Germans moved across the Elbe

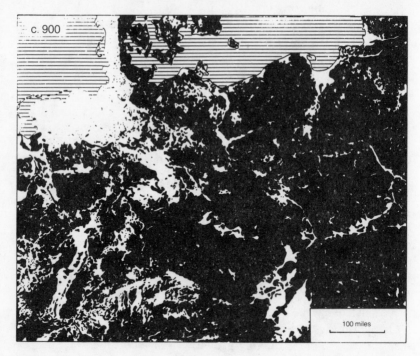

Figure 2.1   The forest area of Central Europe, *c*.900. (*Source*: H. C. Darby, 'The clearing of the woodland in Europe', in W. L. Thomas, Jr (ed.), *Man's Role in Changing the Face of the Earth*, Chicago, 1955, p. 202.)

after about 1150 and eventually settled as far east as the Vistula; these regions were to provide Western and Southern Europe with grain in the sixteenth century. In the south the Spanish slowly reconquered Iberia, which had been occupied by the Moors since the eighth century.

Between 1345 and 1348 the Black Death killed perhaps one-third of the population of Western Europe, and later outbreaks led to a further decline in numbers. The expansion of arable ceased, poorer land was abandoned and much lowland arable was converted to grass. But by the end of the fifteenth century population was growing again, and throughout the sixteenth century much reclamation was carried out, from the embankments of the coast of north Germany to those of Provence and Languedoc. For the first time statistics are available, for the Dutch kept records both of the embankment of coastal polders and of the drainage of interior

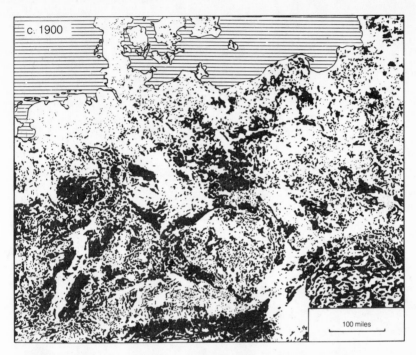

Figure 2.2 The forest area of Central Europe, *c.*1900. (Source: H. C. Darby, 'The clearing of the woodland in Europe', in W. L. Thomas (ed.), *Man's Role in Changing the Face of the Earth*, Chicago, 1955, p. 203.)

lakes, the result of earlier peat diggings (figure 2.3). By the mid-seventeenth century the first serious attempts to drain the English fenlands were undertaken, under Dutch direction.

The great boom in cereal prices finally came to an end in the 1640s; in Southern Europe the population was declining for much of the seventeenth century and in the north it was stable until the 1730s. But except in Germany, where the Thirty Years War reduced the population, the arable area did not decline as it had done after the Black Death, although it was not until population and cereal prices began to rise in the middle of the eighteenth century that the arable area began to expand again and continued to do so until the late nineteenth century. After 1800 estimates of the arable area are available and there is little doubt that there was a marked increase. In Norway and Sweden it doubled in the nineteenth century; in France it rose from 19 million hectares in the 1750s to

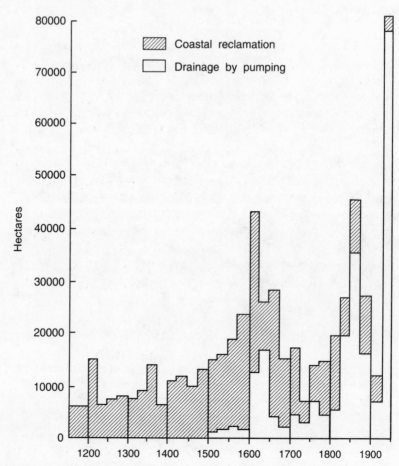

Figure 2.3 Reclamation of coastal polders and internal lakes in the Netherlands, 1100–1950. (*Source*: P. Wagret, *Polderlands*, Methuen, London, 1968, p. 76.)

over 25 million in the 1840s; in Germany east of the Elbe it rose by 73 per cent between 1800 and 1895, and in England it increased by one-quarter between the battle of Waterloo and the Crimean War.

By the end of the nineteenth century the arable area, and indeed the total cultivated area of Western Europe, had reached its peak and there was little reclamation after the 1880s except in northern Scandinavia. This was not so east of the Elbe where there was what amounted to a frontier movement into the Great Afold and the Danubian plains.

The decline of the fallow

Until the middle of the nineteenth century a substantial proportion of the arable area of Western Europe was left in fallow each year. There were two reasons for this. First, during the fallow year the land was rested and nitrogen added to the soil by rain and bacteria, so helping to maintain crop yields. Second, as long as crops were broadcast rather than drilled in rows, the land could only be weeded during a fallow.

Until the eighth century most crops were grown in a two-field system where one was in fallow, the other in crops; each field was thus fallowed every other year. But from the ninth century this began to be replaced in France by the three-field system; this increased the area in crops from 50 to 66 per cent of the arable, but as late as the thirteenth century the three-field system was well established only in parts of the Paris basin, and was only just beginning to replace the two-field system in parts of England.

The fallow in the three-field system began to be eliminated in parts of Flanders in the thirteenth and fourteenth centuries, when legumes and root crops were grown in rotation with cereals. These crops were not grown upon the fallow in England until the mid-seventeenth century. Even then the reduction in the fallow area was slow. At the beginning of the nineteenth century one-fifth of the arable was still, in England, left fallow, and even more in other countries (figure 2.4). By the end of the century, however, the fallow had disappeared, occupied not only by legumes and turnips, but by sugar beet and potatoes, crops which allowed weeding whilst the crop was growing, thus rendering the fallow unnecessary. So between 1000 and 1900 the European sown area was increased substantially, not only by reclaiming new land, but by reducing the fallow. But by the end of the nineteenth century the expansion had ended, partly due to developments in the areas settled by Europeans overseas.

New lands

By the beginning of the twentieth century both the cultivated area and the arable area of Western Europe had reached their maximum. There was little land left to bring into cultivation and gains

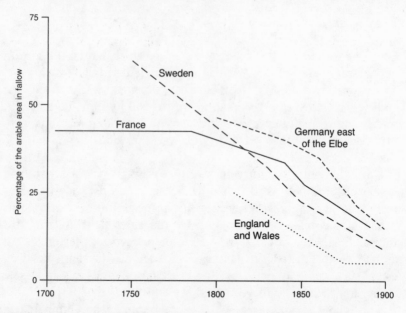

Figure 2.4   The decline in the proportion of arable land in fallow in selected countries, 1700–1900.

from reclamation in Scandinavia and parts of the Mediterranean basin were more than offset by the loss of arable land to urban expansion. This was particularly noticeable in England, Belgium and the Netherlands. Since 1945 Europe's arable area has declined.

But by the nineteenth century Europeans were not confined to thier own continent. They had been settled in the United States and Canada since the seventeenth century; Spaniards, although few in numbers, had settled in the Rio Plata area, since the eighteenth century; Australia was colonized in the late eighteenth century and New Zealand in the 1840s. From the middle of the nineteenth century there was a quite extraordinary expansion of cropland in these countries, and in southern Russia. A frontier of settlement advanced into areas sparsely populated with indigenous peoples, who were treated with scant respect. This great expansion had first begun in the early eighteenth century when Russians moved south to occupy the wooded steppe, and later in the century they colonized the semi-arid grasslands with their fertile *chernozem* soils. In the United States Americans advanced their frontier over the Alleghennies, and from the 1820s drove west, first colonizing the

Table 2.2   The expansion of cropland in Europe, Russia and the
European settlements overseas, 1860–1985 (million hectares)

	1860	1880	1910	1930	1960	1985
United States	65.8	75.9	140.1	166.8	158.3	187.9
Russia	49.2	102.6	114.3	109.4	195.9	232.2
Canada	–	6.1	14.1	23.4	25.0	46.8
Argentina	–	0.4	19.3	24.2	22.2	36.1
Australia	0.4	1.6	4.4	10.1	11.7	48.6
Russia and Europe overseas	115.4	186.6	292.2	333.9	413.1	551.6
Europe	140.0	–	147.0	150.0	151.0	139.6
Total	255.4	–	439.2	483.9	564.1	691.2

Sources: D. Grigg, *The Agricultural Systems of the World*, London, 1974, p. 261;
Food and Agriculture Organization, *Production Yearbook 1986*, 40, Rome, 1986.

wooded areas of the eastern states, and from the 1840s occupying
the grasslands of the Mississippi basin and beyond. By the 1890s
they had reached the Rockies, and the United States Census declared the frontier officially closed. The effective settlement of the
Canadian prairies came later; the wheat acreage was only 1 million
hectares in 1900, 10 million hectares by 1931. The agricultural
settlement of the Argentinian pampas and the Australian interior
also date only from the end of the nineteenth century. Although
grain and cattle had been shipped to Europe from North America
in the late eighteenth century, it was the great expansion of the rail
network in these countries and the fall of oceanic freight rates that
led to the increase in exports of grain, meat and livestock products
in the 1870s and 1880s, threatening the prosperity of West European farmers, who had hitherto imported grain and cattle mainly
from Eastern Europe and Russia.

   This extraordinary growth has dwarfed Europe's arable expansion (table 2.2 and figure 2.5). In the 1860s Europe had a fifth more
arable land than Russia and these overseas countries combined, but
by the eve of the First World War their area was double that of
Europe. Not surprisingly, these vast areas increasingly fed Europe
as well as their own growing home populations, which – with the
exception of Russia – received a great number of migrants from

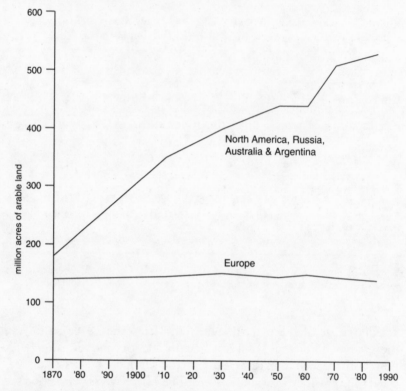

Figure 2.5   The expansion of the arable area in Europe and in other European-settled areas, 1870–1980. (*Source*: D. Grigg, *The Agricultural Systems of the World*, Cambridge, 1974, p. 261; Food and Agriculture Organization, *Production Yearbook 1988*, Rome, vol. 42, 1989, p. 42.)

Europe from the 1880s. By 1985 Europe's arable – no more than it had been in 1860 – was a mere quarter of that of Russia and the overseas countries.

The quality of the land

Not only has the quantity of land been increased, but the quality of much of Europe's arable has been slowly improved. The drainage of low-lying lands has added extra land, but much of this could only be used extensively until after the introduction of steam-pumping in the early nineteenth century ensured that water could be moved from drain to dyke. In Southern Europe traditional farming relied on the winter rainfall to produce cereals harvested in the early summer. Only relatively drought-resistant crops such as olives could survive the hot dry summers. Some irrigation was used, notably in south-eastern Spain, where it had been introduced by the Moors, but the large-scale expansion of irrigation has only occurred in the twentieth century. In the wetter parts of Northern Europe, the quality of heavy clay soils has been slowly improved by underdrainage, which until the nineteenth century was not very effective. The mole-plough and the successful manufacture of clay pipes greatly increased the productivity of these soils, which occupy a considerable area of Northern Europe.

The last two centuries have seen other improvements to the quality of land. The construction of hedges, walls and fences have eased the management of livestock, the boring of wells has allowed the use of semi-arid lands for grazing, and farm roads and farm buildings have been improved. Indeed, capital improvement has made up an increasing proportion of the value of land in this century.

In some areas the improvement in the quality of land has been delayed. In North America and Australia little attention was paid before the 1930s to farming systems that maintained soil fertility, and crop yields were falling in the late nineteenth and early twentieth centuries. By the 1920s land was being lost to soil erosion; it was this that turned the American farmers' attention to the farming practices long established in Western Europe.

Conclusions

Until the nineteenth century most of the extra food needed by a slowly increasing population came from increasing the area in cultivation and increasing the proportion of the arable sown to crops. In the twentieth century output has continued to increase, but mostly from increased yields. European areas overseas have followed a similar course. In the 1860s crop yields in North America were lower than in Western Europe, and showed little change, while the area in crops was greatly increased. Since the 1930s the area in crops has continued to increase – unlike the pattern in Europe – but increased yields have accounted for much of the extra output.

3
Labour

One of the chief characteristics of a traditional society is that the majority of the workforce is employed in agriculture. Because most censuses do not begin until after industrialization had commenced, the precise proportion is not known. In the Swedish census of 1750, 80 per cent were engaged in agriculture, as they were a hundred years later. Historians have estimated the proportion at 80 per cent in France in 1700, 75 per cent in Austria in 1790, 78 per cent in Bohemia in 1756 and 71.9 per cent in the United States in 1820. In the first census in Britain, in 1801, only 36 per cent were recorded as employed in farming, but by then Britain's industrialization was well under way; a recent estimate suggests that 75 per cent of the population were employed in farming in 1600. It seems clear that in most pre-industrial societies three-quarters to four-fifths of the population were engaged in agriculture.

With industrialization the proportion in agriculture declined. Everywhere that industrialization occurred in North America, Western Europe and Australia, the total population increased. Initially the agricultural population also increased, but not so rapidly as the numbers employed in manufacturing, mining and services, so that the percentage engaged in agriculture declined. By 1985 it had fallen below 10 per cent in nearly all Western countries, and in Britain, Belgium and Switzerland to only 2 per cent. However, the real decline in the importance of the agricultural sector was not so great. Many of the activities now carried out by people living off farms were formerly undertaken by farm families, such as transporting goods to market, repairing buildings, wagons and implements, and even making furniture or clothes. Most of the inputs now used on farms, such as fertilizers and machinery, are made by people working in factories, whereas the traditional farmer produced most of his own inputs. Some of the products once processed on the farm, such as cheese and butter, are now made in factories. If those who are engaged in these pursuits are counted, then a much higher proportion of the population is still employed in producing and distributing food and fibre products than these figures suggest. In the United States, only 2 per cent of the total employed population work on farms, but another 20 per cent are also employed in the production and distribution of food and fibres.

There are stages of specialization within the agricultural sector. In the first many non-agricultural tasks are shed, such as mending farm implements, repairing the farm house, and transporting products to market. The farmers concentrate on farming and rural artisans such as wheelwrights, carriers and blacksmiths provide more services. Both increase their productivity by specializing, and the rural economy as a whole gains. This stage has been recognized in the Netherlands in the sixteenth and seventeenth centuries. Later farmers begin to buy inputs from specialist producers rather than making them themselves. In England and France blacksmiths were making agricultural implements as early as the twelfth century; as late as the eighteenth century most implements were still made by local artisans. The agricultural engineering industry did not develop until the 1820s, whilst commercial fertilizer production began only in the 1840s. In the last stage much of the output of the farm is processed in factories rather than on the farm.

The decline of the agricultural population

There are few national statistics on occupational structure before the middle of the nineteenth century. The progress of the decline, and the way in which it occurred at different dates in Western countries, can however be shown by depicting the point at which the proportion engaged in agriculture ceased to be a majority of the working population (figure 3.1). This first occured in Britain in the 1720s but not elsewhere in Europe until the 1840s, when the proportion fell below 50 per cent in Ireland, Belgium and the Netherlands. This stage was not reached in Spain until the 1940s, an indication of how slow the process of industrialization has been in Western Europe. In Britain the proportion employed in agriculture had fallen below 10 per cent before the First World War, but this point was not reached in any other Western country until after the Second World War (figure 3.1), and has not yet been reached in Ireland, Spain and Portugal.

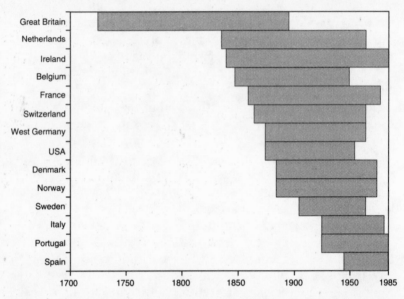

Figure 3.1   The decline in the percentage of the total population engaged
in agriculture. (The left end of the bar shows when the agricultural
population fell below 50 per cent of the workforce; the right end shows
when it fell below 10 per cent.) (*Source*: P. Bairoch, *International Historical
Statistics, vol. I, The Working Population and its Structure*, New York, 1969; Food
and Agriculture Organization, *Production Yearbooks*, Rome.)

The transition from traditional to modern agriculture has begun at
very different dates; and if modernization may be defined as the
impact of industrialization upon agriculture, then it has clearly
taken a very long time. But, of course, the late industrializers have
been able to import fertilizers and machinery from other countries,
and have not had to wait for their own input industries to
develop.

The progress of the agricultural workforce

It has often been assumed that as the proportion of the population
engaged in agriculture declines, so too do the absolute numbers.
This is true today in all developed countries, but over much of the
period of modernization the agricultural labour force has been
increasing or stable, and in many countries absolute decline has

only begun in the last half century. The size of the agricultural work force is a function of a number of factors. First is the rate of natural increase in the agricultural population. As long as the bulk of farmers are peasants any natural increase in the population will be absorbed on farms, for whilst capitalist farmers may hire and fire labourers, peasants do not make their children redundant. Second are the employment opportunities available off the farm. These include jobs in rural areas, which in pre-industrial society would include crafts and services but also some household industrial activities such as weaving and spinning. Far more important in the long run were the economic opportunities created in the towns during the industrialization of the nineteenth century. This included jobs not only in the new factories but also in transport, shops, domestic service, the police and a variety of other non-manufacturing activities. Of those who left French agriculture between 1896 and 1936, only 15 per cent went into manufacturing industry.

There are no statistics for any European country on the size of the agricultural labour force before 1850. However, an estimate of the size of the *rural* population can be made by deducting the numbers of those living in towns of over 10,000 from the total population of the country. This will clearly underestimate the size of the urban population, for many of those in towns under 10,000 will not in any sense be rural, but the trend is probably accurate. Until the eighteenth century the increase in the rural population followed the course of total population increase, for between 1500 and 1800 the percentage living in towns rose only from 5.5 per cent of the total to 11.1 per cent (table 6.1 and figure 3.2). The rural population rose in the sixteenth century, but stagnated or fell in the seventeenth century. In the eighteenth century the total population began to increase rapidly; although this period saw the beginning of urbanization, the rural population also rose, dramatically: between 1750 and 1890 the rural population of Western Europe doubled. In both the sixteenth and the nineteenth centuries the growth of rural population caused the subdivision and fragmentation of farms, increased landlessness, reduced the real wages of labourers and retarded the adoption of labour-saving implements and machines. By the 1850s agricultural underemployment was widespread in West European countries: that is to say, there were far more people living on farms than were needed to carry out farming tasks. This

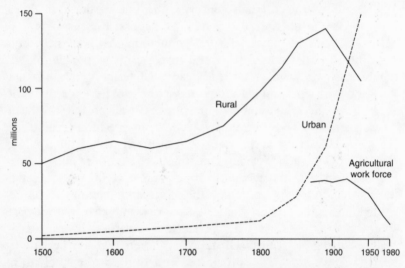

Figure 3.2   The rural and urban populations of Western Europe, 1500–1980. 'Urban' indicates the population in places of more than 10,000. (*Source*: J. De Vries, *European Urbanization 1600–1800*, London, 1984.)

condition persisted in most parts of Western Europe until the 1940s. On the other hand the abundance and cheapness of labour allowed the clearance of new land, made possible the improvement of land by draining and underdraining, and also made easier the construction of roads, fences, walls and farm buildings. Most important, it allowed more intensive farming practices. Crop yields were increased by more ploughings, frequent weeding and the use of labour-intensive crops such as sugar beet, turnips and potatoes. In many parts of Europe labour abundance allowed the switch to higher-value systems such as viticulture and horticulture.

Growth and decline

In the eighteenth and for much of the nineteenth century the fertility of rural was higher than that of urban populations, and urban mortality higher than rural, and so natural increase in the countryside exceeded that of the towns. Although there was – and always had been – migration from rural to urban areas, it was less than natural increase, so rural population carried on increasing.

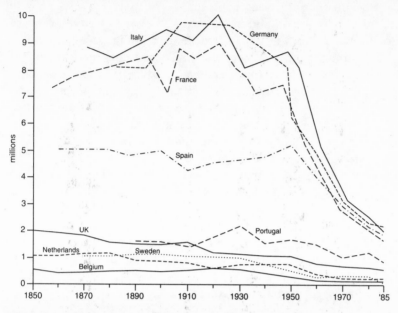

Figure 3.3 The agricultural labour force (men and women) in selected
West European countries, 1850–1985. (*Source*: P. Bairoch, *International
Historical Statistics, vol. I, The Working Population and its Structure*, New York,
1969; Food and Agriculture Organization, *Production Yearbooks*, Rome.)

Some of this increase was absorbed in rural industries in the seventeenth, eighteenth and early nineteenth centuries, a process described by some historians as proto-industrialization; consequently
agriculture did not have to absorb all rural population increase.
Nonetheless between 1750 and 1850 the agricultural workforce of
Western Europe continued to increase. There then came a major
change; the continued outflow from the rural areas began to equal
or exceed the natural increase and the agricultural labour force
entered a long period of stagnation or, in a few countries, began
a long decline (figure 3.3). There were many reasons for this. In
Scandinavia, Italy and Ireland emigration overseas was of prime
importance. In France the continued decline of fertility was significant. But most important was the great increase in employment
opportunities in the mining and manufacturing areas, beginning
first in Britain, then Belgium, and later in Switzerland, France and
Germany. The towns offered jobs, and generally at wages above
those in agriculture. For most of the nineteenth and much of the

early twentieth century agricultural wages in England were only half those in industry, and in the first half of the twentieth century agricultural incomes in the United States were only 40 per cent of those in non-agricultural occupations. There were other reasons for the rural exodus. In the late eighteenth and early nineteenth centuries enclosure may have impoverished the small landowners, who had to bear part of the cost and so were forced to sell; though this affected only England (and then mainly before 1820), Denmark and Sweden. The loss of common rights would have impoverished those with only a cottage or garden, and they too might have left for the towns. Later in the nineteenth century the other amenities of the city, notably better education and better entertainments, proved a powerful attraction. In some farming areas in the later nineteenth and early twentieth centuries farmers may have purchased machines to rid themselves of labourers. But without doubt the major factors in accounting for the decline of the agricultural labour force were the employment opportunities in the towns and the higher wages to be found there.

The differential chronology of decline

The agricultural workforce of Western Europe reached a peak in the 1850s; there was only a slight increase thereafter. But there was a great difference between countries in the date when decline began. The agricultural population of Britain declined from the 1850s (figure 3.3), that of France and Germany from the end of the nineteenth century; in Southern Europe agricultural populations did not reach their peak until well into the twentieth century, for industrialization and urbanization were later here than in the rest of Western Europe. But until the 1920s the rate of decline in the agricultural population was slow everywhere except in Britain and Ireland. In 1870 the agricultural workforce of Western Europe was about 38 million; it reached a peak of 41 million in 1921 and had fallen to 31 million by 1950. Since then, however, the fall has been precipitous: in 1985 only 10 million worked on the land (figures 3.2 and 3.3).

All European settlements overseas have gone through a similar sequence – a period of increasing agricultural population followed by slow and then rapid decline – and the reasons have been much

the same as in Western Europe. But there is an important difference. From the late nineteenth century these countries – the
United States in particular – were receiving large numbers of
immigrants; more importantly their agricultural frontiers continued
to expand, in contrast with Europe, until well into the 1930s. The
post-war period has also seen a continued expansion (above, table
2.2) of the arable area. Consequently the decline in the agricultural
labour force set in somewhat later than in most of Western Europe.
In the United States it began in the First World War, but in
Canada, Australia, New Zealand and Argentina not until after the
Second.

The decline of the agricultural population in both Western
Europe and North America has been selective. Although the family
farm, which does not have hired labour, has been most characteristic, there have also been some areas where hired labourers have
been important, notably in England, Germany east of the Elbe, and
northern France. Until the 1950s most of the decline in the numbers in agriculture was due to the emigration of farm workers, not
farmers. But since the end of the Second World War farmers as
well as workers have left the land; farmers with small holdings have
given up, and children have left the family farm and not returned
when their father has died or retired. There has also been a particular tendency for the young, and particularly young men, to leave
agriculture, so that the modern agricultural labour force is older
than the non-agicultural labour force and women are a comparatively high and increasing percentage of it (table 3.1).

The consequences of decline

In Europe, the date at which the decline of the agricultural population began had an influence on the rate of mechanization in farming. In Britain a continuous decline in the labour force began in the
1850s, and the mechanization of cereal production got under way
long before it did in the rest of Europe, where the decline in the
agricultural population began later. Even in the 1950s a considerable proportion of the agricultural workforce of Western Europe
was underemployed, and this surplus had long retarded the rate of
mechanization. More dramatic was the difference between the densities of the agricultural population of Western Europe on the one

Table 3.1 Age and sex structure of the agricultural labour force in the European Economic Community

	Percentage over 45, 1980		Women as a percentage of agricultural labour force, 1977
	In agriculture	In total labour force	
West Germany	53.1	33.7	49.1
France	60.7	34.5	33.9
Italy	59.1	35.9	29.5
Netherlands	45.5	28.4	8.0
Belgium	53.0	31.0	22.1
Britain	45.4	37.4	17.6
Ireland	57.3	31.3	8.3
Denmark	54.5	33.3	19.2
Total	56.4	34.9	31.6

Source: Eurostats.

hand and of the European-settled regions overseas on the other: in the 1850s agricultural population densities in Western Europe were two or three times those in the coastal regions of North America. There was also a great difference in their resource endowment. In Western Europe most of the land that could be cultivated was already in farmland by then. In contrast, in North America a great area of potential arable lay to the west, but there was a shortage of labour. From the 1820s the frontier of settlement moved westwards across the United States, always in conditions of labour shortage; and although in Western Europe the agricultural population slowly declined, the gap in population densities between the two continents persisted. This difference led to quite different pathways of agricultural development after 1850. In the United States – and later in Canada, Australia and New Zealand – wages were high but land was cheap, so farmers tried to maximize the use of their scarcest resource, labour, by substituting machines for men. In Western Europe labour was not in short supply, but land was, so farmers aimed at maximizing output per hectare, trying to increase crop yields by frequent cultivation, much weeding, the use of manure and, later, chemical fertilizers, and adopting intensive live-stock production systems.

Conclusion

In traditional agriculture the main factors of production were land and labour. Until the nineteenth century the course of the agricultural population followed closely that of the population in general. Both populations increased in the nineteenth century, but immigration to the towns first stabilized and then slowly reduced agricultural populations. Differences in agricultural population density have led to different types of development, with the high density countries of Western Europe seeking to maximize output per hectare, and the low-density countries of North America and Australia aiming to maximize output per man.

4

The Productivity of Land

The great changes in farming in the last two centuries have produced increases not only in output but also in productivity; farmers have increased the output they get from each unit of resource used. This increase in productivity is not easy to measure. Conventionally two indices are used: labour productivity, or output per man, and land productivity, or output per hectare of agricultural land, which is dealt with in this chapter. Until the eighteenth century most of the increased output came from expanding the area in cultivation, and land productivity increased very little; indeed, some historians believe it was static from the Middle Ages to the nineteenth century. But in the twentieth century most of the extra output has come, not from expanding area, but from increased output per hectare.

Measuring crop yields

The ideal measure of output per hectare is the *value* of all output, including both crop and livestock production. Sadly, such data are not usually available today, and rarely for the past, so that historians have had to rely upon crop yields. Because wheat was the most important crop in the past, there are more records of its yield than for other crops, and so wheat yield is used as a measure of land productivity. National records of average wheat yield only exist from the late nineteenth century; before then, records of yield generally only exist for single years, or for particular estates or indeed individual farms. Not surprisingly, because of the paucity of information, there has been much debate about the trend of crop yields before the nineteenth century. There are two ways of measuring crop yields. Modern estimates are of the average weight or volume of grain harvested per hectare; medieval and early modern estimates are often seed yield ratios, that is the ratio between the

weight or volume of seed sown and the amount harvested per
hectare.

Crop yields before 1850

As mentioned above, the scarcity of reliable information on wheat
yields in Europe before 1850 has led to considerable debate. In
England there is some agreement that the average yield was about
670–800 kg per hectare in the thirteenth, fourteenth and fifteenth
centuries, although higher yields were obtained in East Anglia, as
they were in northern France and the Low Countries; nor does
there seem to have been much increase before the seventeenth
century. Thereafter there is much disagreement. It used to be
thought that yields only began to increase in England and France
after the mid-eighteenth century, the period once described as the
'agricultural revolution'. However, some historians now believe
that yields in England began to increase in the seventeenth century.
One estimate puts the national average at 670 kg per hectare in
1650, 1210 kg in 1750, 1340–1410 kg in 1800 and 1880 kg in 1850.
There is, however, little doubt that yields doubled between the
mid-seventeenth and the mid-nineteenth century. In France there
has also been vigorous debate, with some contending that the late
eighteenth century saw an upturn in yields, and others denying that
any change occurred before the 1840s. B. H. Slicher van Bath has
assembled evidence on seed yield ratios in Europe from the sixteenth to the early nineteenth century, which suggest that England
and the Low Countries has the highest yields throughout the period
(table 4.1) and also experienced the greatest increase in the early
modern period.

Yields since the nineteenth century

Records of wheat yields are more accurate from the late nineteenth
century as national agricultural statistics become available. In the
middle of the nineteenth century the average yield in Western
Europe was probably only 1 tonne per hectare; since then it has
risen fourfold (table 4.2), and in some countries more dramatically:
fivefold in the Netherlands and France and sixfold in Germany

Table 4.1   Seed/yield ratios[a] in the regions of Europe, 1500–1820

	1	2	3	4
1500–49	7.4	6.7	4.0	3.9
1550–99	7.3	–	4.4	4.3
1600–49	6.7	–	4.5	4.0
1650–99	9.3	6.2	4.1	3.8
1700–49	–	6.3	4.1	3.5
1750–99	10.1	7.0	5.1	4.7
1800–20	11.1	6.2	5.4	–

Zone 1: England, The Low Countries
Zone 2: France, Spain, Italy
Zone 3: Germany, Switzerland, Scandinavia
Zone 4: Russia, Poland, Czechoslovakia, Hungary
[a] For barley, wheat, oats and rye.
Source: B. H. Slicher van Bath, 'Agriculture in the vital revolution', in E. E. Rich and C. H. Wilson (eds), *The Cambridge Economic History of Europe, vol. 5: The Economic Organization of Early Modern Europe*, Cambridge, 1977, p. 81.

(figure 4.1). Between the 1880s and the 1930s increases were relatively modest, only 20 per cent in Western Europe as a whole (table 4.2), but doubling in Sweden and Germany (figure 4.1). Since the 1930s, however, there has been a prodigious increase. In Western Europe wheat yields have tripled since the 1930s (table 4.2). Indeed, yields have doubled in the last twenty-five years alone, an increase greater than that achieved in Western Europe in the 550 years between 1300 and 1850.

In the areas settled by Europeans overseas, yields were and are lower than in Western Europe and increased only slowly until the 1930s (table 4.2 and figure 4.1); indeed, they actually declined in the early twentieth century. Since the 1930s, as in Western Europe, they have increased remarkably and the difference between the two regions has greatly diminished (table 4.2).

What causes increases in crop yields?

Some of the more important determinants of crop yields – solar radiation, temperature and rainfall – have not changed greatly over

Table 4.2 Wheat yields in Western Europe, North America, Australia
and Argentina, 1885–1986 (metric tonnes per hectare)

	(A) Western Europe	(B) Europe Overseas	(B) as a % age of (A)
1885–89	1.1	0.7	63.5
1889–94	1.1	0.8	72.7
1894–99	1.2	0.8	66.6
1899–1904	1.2	0.8	66.6
1904–09	1.2	0.9	75.0
1909–14	1.3	0.9	69.2
1914–19	1.3	0.9	69.2
1919–24	1.3	0.8	61.5
1924–29	1.3	0.9	69.2
1929–34	1.35	0.8	59.3
1934–37	1.35	0.7	51.8
1948–52	1.6	1.1	68.8
1961–65	2.2	1.5	68.2
1979–81	3.7	3.3	89.2
1986	4.0	3.7	92.5

(A) Austria, Belgium, United Kingdom, Ireland, Czechoslovakia, Denmark,
Finland, France, Germany, Greece, Italy, Netherlands, Norway, Portugal, Spain,
Sweden, Switzerland.
(B) USA, Canada, Argentina, Australia.
Sources: W. Mandelbaum, *The World Wheat Economy 1885–1939*, Cambridge, MA,
1953, pp. 240–1; Food and Agriculture Organization, *Production Yearbooks*, Rome.

the last millennium. For most farmers the principal factor is the
supply of plant nutrients – nitrogen, phosphorus, potassium – in
the soil. Under natural vegetation there is a cycle of nutrients
between vegetation and soil; vegetation decays, nutrients return to
the soil and thence to the vegetation, so the biomass is stable over
long periods. But when farming is established not only is the
natural vegetation – a source of nutrients for the soil – removed,
but each harvest removes nutrients in the harvested grass and crop.
Thus the central problem of farming is how to maintain, and
ideally increase, the supply of nutrients in the soil. Crop yields
are, however, not a function of the plant nutrient supply alone. A
fertile soil supplies nutrients for weeds as well as crops and so
reduces yields, and crops can be damaged or destroyed by disease.

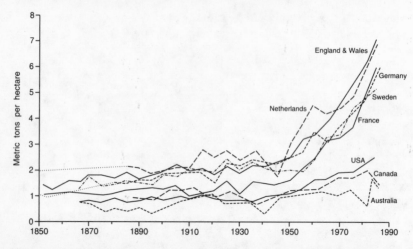

Figure 4.1   Wheat yields in selected countries, 1850–1985. (*Source*: D. Grigg, *The Dynamics of Agricultural Change: The Historical Experience*, London, 1982, p. 130; Food and Agriculture Organization, *Production Yearbooks, 1988*, vol. 42, Rome, 1989.)

Three different farming systems have existed in Western Europe to undertake the tasks of supplying nutrients and controlling weeds and disease: the open-field farming of medieval and early modern times; mixed farming, which replaced open-field farming in much of Western Europe in the eighteenth and nineteenth centuries; and the chemical farming of modern times, which has its beginnings in the mid-nineteenth century but has replaced mixed farming only since the 1950s.

The traditional farming of the medieval and early modern period

The open-field system prevailed over much of Northern Europe in the later Middle Ages. Arable land was divided into a number of large fields – from two to six – of which one would be in fallow each year. Autumn and spring cereals were grown and a small amount of peas and beans. Crops were sown broadcast, not in rows, and the land was ploughed before sowing with a cumbersome wooden plough drawn by oxen. Livestock grazed on poor grassland which was held in common, on the stubble left after harvest, and on fallow land.

Table 4.3 Nitrogen inputs in a crop fallow system

	Kg per hectare
Rain, dust	8–12
Seed	4
Manure	5
Free-living bacteria	2–5
Legumes[a]	20–40
Leguminous weeds	2–10
	41–76

[a] Assuming 10% of the arable was in peas and beans.
Source: R. S. Loomis, 'Ecological dimensions of medieval agrarian systems: an ecologist responds', *Agricultural History*, 52 (1978), 478–83.

This farming system was characterized by low crop yields for three reasons. First, the nitrogen cycle operated at a low level. Nitrogen was acquired in the fallow year from rain, from the action of free-living bacteria in the soil, from the small area of legumes – mainly peas and beans – that were grown and from the limited amount of animal dung available. R. S. Loomis has calculated that a cereal yield of 1000 kg per hectare would mean a loss of 20 kg of nitrogen per hectare, but that during a year in the crop and a year in fallow, enough nitrogen would have been obtained to replace this loss (table 4.3). Inefficient weeding also helped to ensure that yields were low, and lower than the average nitrogen cycle would have allowed. Autumn ploughings were done in a great hurry. Because seed was broadcast it was not possible to weed during crop growth, and so a fallow was needed to ensure that weeds were removed. Yields were further reduced by pests and disease, against which traditional farmers had little protection, though as most plant diseases are specific to individual species the use of fallow may have limited the build-up of soil-borne disease.

The rise of mixed farming

The traditional farming of the open fields was slowly replaced by mixed farming whose essence was that crops which increased the

Table 4.4   Nitrogen supply, kg/ha of arable land

	c.1770	1880
Seed	1.8	2.1
Farmyard manure	8.3	17.4
Legume residues	–	5.7–8.2
Other biological fixation	16.0	16.0
Atmospheric fixation	3.5	4.5
Commercial fertilizer	–	1.0
Total	29.6	46.7–49.2

Source: G. P. H. Chorley, 'The agricultural revolution in Northern Europe, 1750–1880; nitrogen, legumes and crop productivity', *Economic History Review*, 34 (1981), 71–93.

supply of fodder were grown upon the fallow. This increased the number of animals which could be kept and hence the supply of manure, and so increased crop yields. Root crops began to be grown upon the fallow – turnips, swedes, potatoes, sugar beet – which, if drilled in rows, allowed the crop to be horse- or hand-hoed during growth and thus reduced the need for fallowing. In addition, the fodder roots could be fed to livestock, as could damaged potatoes and the tops and residues of sugar beet. From the eighteenth century cattle were kept in stalls upon straw, the mixture of straw, urine and faeces providing farmyard manure that could be carted to the fields. Turnips were eaten off *in situ* in the fields by sheep, and their dung enriched the soil. Part of the fallow was devoted to swards which included clover, sown for a year and followed by cereals. This provided grazing that dunged the land, and the clover added nitrogen to the soil. Indeed, this was a prime cause of the increase in the nitrogen supply in Western Europe soils between 1770 to 1880 and thus a major factor in the increase in crop yields at that time (table 4.4). The new crops – roots and clover – were grown in rotation with cereals, which may have helped control plant disease. Other improvements took place at the same time. Lime was used to reduce acidity, which in turn increased the activity of nitrogen-fixing bacteria, and a variety of fertilizers such as marl and bone increased crop yields. The slow improvement of implements – particularly the plough and harrow

– increased the efficiency of weeding, as did the adoption of the seed drill in the nineteenth century.

The chronology of the spread of mixed farming

Mixed farming was a package of innovations; if only one of its techniques or crops were adopted the effect upon crop yields was limited, but the full integration of crop and livestock husbandry produced farming systems that gave average wheat yields of about 2000 kg per hectare, two or three times that typical of traditional farming. It is, however, difficult to trace the spread of individual innovations, even more so that of the package. Turnips and clover began to be grown in the Low Countries in the late Middle Ages; in England their use dates from the mid-seventeenth century, but they were not properly integrated into a rotation until the nineteenth century. The seed drill was not widely employed in Western Europe until the mid-nineteenth century; indeed, in many places it did not replace broadcasting until much later. Mixed farming as an integrated system took hold in eastern England in the later eighteenth century, but in France in the 1840s was still confined to parts of the Paris basin. The adoption of clover came mainly after 1770. Only 4 per cent of the arable of North-West Europe was in clover in the 1770s, but 19 per cent by 1880.

Thus the beginnings of mixed husbandry can be traced back to the late medieval period. It developed in the Low Countries in the sixteenth and seventeenth centuries, then spread in England in the late seventeenth and eighteenth centuries, reaching its apogee in the High Farming of early Victorian times. Adopted later in the rest of Europe, it spread rapidly in the nineteenth century. By the 1930s it was the dominant system in Western Europe; in contrast, much of Eastern Europe was still characterized by the dominance of cereal growing and the failure to integrate crop and livestock production on the same farm.

Farming in the European-settled areas overseas

Until the nineteenth century, Europeans in North America were still found mainly east of the Appalachians and the Great Lakes;

Australia was not colonized until 1786 and until the 1860s arable farming was restricted to the coastal areas. Nowhere in North America or Australia were there the high population densities characteristic of Western Europe. Although European crops and livestock were grown in these new lands – maize, tobacco and potatoes were the only significant additions – farming methods were very different. Farms were larger and less labour was available, so farming was less intensive. Because farmers knew there was abundant land in the interior little attempt was made to conserve soil fertility, integrate crop and livestock production, or pursue the labour-intensive practices that increased yields. Rotations were unusual, little manure was used and legumes were uncommon. Thomas Jefferson wrote that he did not use manure 'because we can buy an acre of new land cheaper than we can manure an old acre'. When Americans crossed the Appalachians, they found land that initially was of very high fertility and with apparently unlimited reserves to the west. In the late eighteenth and early nineteenth centuries the major influence on American farming was the writings of British improvers. But although Americans adopted British livestock and implements, they made little attempt to adopt labour-intensive practices or aim at the maintenance of soil fertility. Indeed, as late as the 1920s wheat yields were little above those of the early nineteenth century. Although chemical fertilizers began to be used on the exhausted cotton soils of the south-east in the 1870s, they were little used elsewhere; in the Prairies in 1900 the average expenditure upon fertilizers was less than half a cent per hectare.

From the 1860s many American scientific writers were advocating the use of rotations, manures and fertilizers, but it was the falling crop yields in the Corn Belt and the Prairies in the late nineteenth century that turned the attention of farmers in North America and Australia to mixed farming. Mixed farming began to be pursued in Ontario in the 1870s. In Australia the abundance of land meant that farmers followed much the same course as in the United States; wheat farming expanded in the 1870s on large farms with low yields, using the fallow rather than manure, and little fertilizer was used. However, in the twentieth century farmers in the Australian wheat belt turned to mixed farming as a result of falling yields. The value of imported legumes, particularly subterranean clover, was recognized in the 1890s, but their use was not widely adopted until the 1950s. Wheat in Australia is now grown in rotation with clover, on which sheep are grazed. Comparatively little chemical fertilizer is used, and so the principles of mixed farming, belatedly adopted, are still followed.

The beginnings of modernization: fertilizers

The last thirty years have seen the rapid adoption of chemical fertilizers which have supplemented, or in some cases replaced, the use of livestock manure, of herbicides that destroy weeds and make the hoeing of root crops unnecessary, and of pesticides that have replaced the use of fallow and rotations in controlling disease. Mixed farming has given way to modern chemical farming. But the beginning of this system has a long history.

The use of farmyard manure and legumes to increase crop yields was the key to the spread of mixed farming, and until the 1930s farmyard manure provided most of the plant nutrients added to the soil in Western Europe. Chemical fertilizers only overtook manure as a source of nutrients in Britain in the 1960s, but their use dates back to 1842. In that year J. B. Lawes opened a superphosphate factory in Kent, in which bones were dissolved in sulphuric acid. The use of superphosphate became common in much of Western Europe. Nitrogen was obtained from the import of guano from Peru and later saltpetre from Chile; and by the end of the century sulphate of ammonia, a by-product of gas production, was used in many countries. In the 1860s potash salts began to be mined at Stassfurt in Germany. In the 1880s basic slag, a by-product of the Thomas-Gilchrist steel process, began to be used. By 1900 Britain had been overtaken in the consumption of fertilizer; the highest rates of application were found in Germany, Belgium and the Netherlands. German rates were three times those in France, whilst hardly any fertilizer was used in Italy.

But before the First World War, farmyard manure remained by far the most important source of plant nutrients. It was not until the 1930s that fertilizer consumption began to increase rapidly. This was largely due to the Haber-Bosch method of fixing nitrogen from the atmosphere to give nitrates which could be used as a ferti- lizer, discovered in Germany before the First World War and rapidly adoped elsewhere in Europe in the 1920s and the 1930s. After the Second World War cheap petroleum and gas prices reduced the

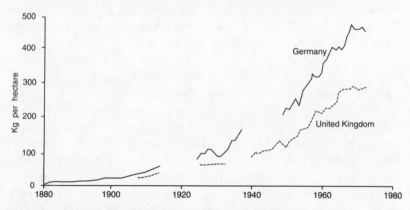

Figure 4.2 Fertilizer consumption per hectare of arable land, Germany (West Germany after 1945) and the United Kingdom. (*Source*: D. Andrews, M. Mitchell and A. Weber, *The Development of Agriculture in Germany and the UK: 3, Comparative Time Series, 1870–1975*, Wye College, Ashford, Kent, 1979.)

real cost of nitrogen fertilizer, and consumption per hectare rose rapidly (figure 4.2). Although farmyard manure remains important in much of Western Europe, it has been overtaken by chemical fertilizers. In the 1970s chemical fertilizers provided 75 per cent of the nitrogen applied to British soils, and 92 per cent of that in the United States. The world's consumption of chemical fertilizers increased sevenfold between 1950 and 1980.

Improved varieties

In traditional agriculture, farmers got their seed from their own harvest and selected that which appeared to yield best. Seed merchants did not appear in Western Europe until the eighteenth century. More important than empirical selection of better seed was the transfer of crops from one region to another. Western Europe benefited from the import of crops indigenous to the Americas, particularly potatoes and maize but also tomatoes and tobacco. In the nineteenth century, European vineyards were restocked with imported American vines after the devastations of *phylloxera* which began in the 1860s.

North America and Australia also benefited from such transfers. The Canadian Prairies had a very short growing season and few of the wheat varieties available in North America in the mid-nineteenth century would mature there; however, Red Fife, a Russian wheat, was taken to Ontario via Scotland in 1842 and later in the century allowed the exploitation of the Prairies. It was replaced before the First World War by an even more rapidly growing variety, Marquis, which had been locally bred.

Equally dramatic were the wheats brought by Mennonites from southern Russia when they emigrated to the United States; they were adapted to a dry regime, and made possible the settlement of the drier Great Plains in the 1870s. In the 1920s cold-tolerant wheats bred in the USSR were imported, and by 1940 they accounted for 40 per cent of the wheat area of the United States.

The nineteenth century saw improvements in crop varieties in Western Europe; in Germany, for example, the sugar content of sugar beet was very nearly doubled between the 1870s and 1910. But more effective breeding of new varieties had to await a proper understanding of plant genetics. The key to this was Gregor Mendel's work in the 1860s, which however did not become generally known until the first decade of this century. Plant-breeding institutes were then established and produced a succession of new varieties that helped increase crop yields by selecting for tolerance of disease, drought and cold. The first major advance was the breeding of hybrid corn in the 1920s. In the 1940s work on wheat produced dwarf varieties capable of absorbing large amounts of fertilizer. More sophisticated breeding has produced varieties adapted to mechanization, such as cotton bolls that open at the same time, tomatoes of the same size, and dwarf apple trees. The breeding of new varieties has made a major contribution to the increased crop yields of the last fifty years. Experiments in the United States and the United Kingdom suggest that half the yield increase in wheat between the 1930s and 1970s, and 20–40 per cent of the corn increases, was due to new varieties, and in Australia 20–25 per cent of wheat increases in the post-war period.

Controlling weeds and disease

Farmers in both past and present spend a great deal of their time and money trying to protect their crops from weeds, insects, fungi and other pests. Weeds use nutrients that could be going to increase crop yields whilst pests damage the growing plant. The immensity of the problem is indicated by the fact that crops in the United States are attacked by 160 bacteria, 250 viruses, 8000 pathogenic fungi, 8000 species of insects and 2000 species of weeds; in 1974 one-third of the United States' potential crop was lost before harvest and in 1981 it was estimated that 45 per cent of the potential world crop output was lost to pests before harvest.

Not surprisingly, traditional farmers, whether using the open-field or mixed system, spent much time trying to eliminate weeds. This was done when ploughing to create a seed bed, and by weeding by horse-hoe or hand. It relied upon a large reservoir of cheap labour. Pests were more difficult to control. Mammals and birds could be shot or snared, but there was little protection against virus, fungi or bacteria. The use of fallow, rotations and leys may have exercised some control.

The first attempts to control pesticides by chemical sprays came in the 1860s, when sprays were used to limit the Colorado beetle which damaged the potato crop in the United States, and vine mildew in France. By 1900 chemical sprays based upon organic toxins such as nicotine and derris were in use, but mainly on high-value products such as fruit and vegetables. In the 1920s some fruit was sprayed by aeroplane in both the United States and the United Kingdom. By the 1930s chemical companies recognized a potentially profitable market, but it was the discovery of DDT in Switzerland in 1939 and of 2,4-D in the United States during the Second World War that paved the way for the growing use of herbicides, fungicides and insecticides. The use of pesticides doubled in the United States between 1964 and 1984, and in the United Kingdom the value of pesticide output quadrupled between 1950 and 1979. As with chemical fertilizers, the use of chemical sprays has a long history, but it is only since the 1950s that their use has become general.

The use of chemicals has had a profound effect upon the organization of agriculture, by making the system of mixed farming unnecessary. Pesticides can control disease, so many farmers have not felt it necessary to practise crop rotation. Chemical fertilizer can replace farmyard manure, so making it unnecessary to keep livestock. Herbicides kill weeds, and consequently there is no need for row crops or for hand-weeding. When evidence in the 1940s showed that the principal value of ploughing in autumn or spring is to kill weeds, the availability of herbicides led many farmers in the United States – and to a lesser extent in Western Europe – to reduce cultivation greatly, abandon the mouldboard plough, and only till the soil lightly with a cultivator. In the space of thirty years the entire basis of mixed farming has been undermined.

Conclusions

Crop yields have shown a remarkable increase over the last 350 years; the average English wheat yield in the 1980s was three times what it was in the 1930s, five times what it was in 1800 and ten times that of 1300. These increases in yield have been achieved first by the replacement of open-field farming by mixed farming, and then by the replacement of mixed farming by modern chemical farming.

But of course there were not distinct periods when only one system predominated. Much of England still lay in open fields and practised traditional farming in the middle of the eighteenth century, although in the enclosed areas mixed farming predominated. Much of France was still following the farming methods of the medieval period when the first sprays and chemical fertilizers were used in the Bordeaux area in the 1860s. Thus both the spread of mixed farming and of modern chemical farming has proceeded very slowly. Mixed farming, although it had been practised in some regions since the seventeenth century, did not reach its peak until the nineteenth century, while modern chemical farming has only replaced mixed farming since the 1950s, although it had its beginnings in the 1840s.

5

The Productivity of Labour

Throughout North America, Western Europe and Australia the agricultural labour force has been declining sharply since the 1950s; people have been replaced by machines. The result has been a dramatic increase in labour productivity or output per man. For many people this has been the chief triumph of modernization and contrasts with traditional agriculture which was labour-intensive, dependent upon human and animal power, and often had to support more people than were needed to carry out the tasks on the farm. Much of the increase in output in traditional farming was obtained by extra labour, either in reclaiming new land or by more intensive practices that increased yields. Thus the traditional farmer was constantly facing the prospect of diminishing returns to labour: each extra hour worked did not bring forth a proportionate increase in output, and average output per head was always threatening to decline. In a peasant society concerned primarily with producing an adequate food supply and avoiding risk this was not seen as a problem; but as soon as produce was sold, and more particularly when labour was hired for wages, economies in labour – or as least the more adroit deployment of labour – began to be important. Traditional farmers were capable of putting off the onset of diminishing returns by adopting new farming practices; but as long as the agricultural population was stable or increasing and absorbed most of its own natural increase, there was little incentive to adopt labour-saving methods because the cost of labour was so low. The onset of mechanization was precipitated by two events. First, in the early nineteenth century the frontier of settlement advanced into unsettled land in North America and Australia, and the combination of abundant land and a sparse population prompted both the invention and adoption of labour-saving machines. Second, in Western Europe the outflow of migrants to the towns eventually exceeded the natural increase of the agricultural population; and as the labour force declined so farmers had to turn to machinery. Because industrialization and migration from the countryside to the towns began first in Britain, it was in Britain that mechanization first occurred in Europe, although it proceeded less rapidly than in North America or Australasia.

Labour productivity in traditional agriculture

It is difficult to trace increases in labour productivity in European agriculture before the nineteenth century, but certainly it seems to have occurred, most notably in England, where agricultural output at least doubled between 1650 and 1850 but without a commensurate increase in the labour force. Changes in the sources of power and type of implements also occurred before the age of mechanization.

Before the nineteenth century power on farms depended entirely upon human and animal muscle. Other forms of power, the windmill and running water, were applied only to processing food and draining marsh and fen. However, there were important changes in the source of traction. The early medieval farmer relied solely upon oxen to draw his plough, harrow and farm wagons, but in the twelfth century the horse began to be used in parts of the Paris basin. This in turn was the result of the earlier introduction of horse-shoes and the horse-collar. Horses seem initially to have been used primarily for harrowing, and their spread was remarkably slow; oxen remained the major source of power on farms in North America and Western Europe until well into the nineteenth century. In England the substitution of the ox by the horse on farms began in the sixteenth century, and accelerated in the seventeenth and eighteenth centuries; by the beginning of the nineteenth century, oxen were rare. The horse was not more powerful than the ox, but it was faster. As long as the open fields persisted and most of the cultivation was for cereals, speed was not of great importance. But when crops began to be grown upon the fallow, the farmers' year was more crowded and speed became a requirement. The horse replaced the ox in the Netherlands in the eighteenth and nineteenth centuries, and in the United States oxen were replaced by horses and mules between 1820 and 1870.

Farmers could also make gains in labour productivity by improving the implements they used. The medieval mouldboard plough was extraordinarily cumbersome, and in the following centuries was slowly improved. In the eighteenth century iron began to be used, and by the 1770s an all-iron plough was manufactured. Indeed, in England agriculture was an important market for the new iron industry, probably taking a third of its output in the eighteenth century. Other implements were simple; some farmers dragged thorn branches across the seed bed rather than using a harrow, whilst others broke the clods with mattocks until the roller was adopted. Harvesting was done by hand; the wheat crop was cut with the sickle, grass with the scythe. Replacing the sickle by the scythe produced important gains in efficiency. In the United States a man with a sickle could cut three-quarters of an acre of wheat in a day; the scythe with a cradle, a wooden attachment that laid the grain in rows, raised this to two acres. Surprisingly, it was only in the nineteenth century, the period of first mechanization, that the sickle was finally replaced by the scythe in harvesting wheat. As the yield and acreage of wheat increased after the end of the Napoleonic Wars, farmers in many parts of Western Europe suffered from labour shortages in the harvesting season; one solution, before the adoption of the reaper, was the substitution of the scythe for the sickle.

Power and modernization

The nineteenth century was the age of steam, which revolutionized factory production, eventually replaced the sail on ships, and on rails superseded, for a while, road and canal transport. Many hoped it would revolutionize agriculture, but its impact was limited, largely because steam power could not easily be harnessed to pull ploughs or other implements. The stationary steam engine was first used in agriculture in 1798 to drive the threshing machine, itelf only invented in 1780s. By the 1880s steam-driven machines threshed most of British grain production, but they were more slowly adopted elsewhere. In Germany in 1907 threshing machines had replaced the flail, but only one-third were steam-driven.

In Britain in the 1840s there were many experiments with steam-powered ploughing. In most of the systems a stationary steam traction engine pulled a plough with hawsers; but in Britain less

Table 5.1 Percentage of horse-power hours worked, USA

	Inanimate	Work animals	Human
1850	5.8	78.8	15.4
1943	94.0	3.0	3.0

Source: E. W. Zimmerman, *World Resources and Industries*, London, 1951, p. 58.

than 1 per cent of arable land was ever ploughed in this way, and the steam plough made little headway elsewhere, except in the United States and Germany. Towards the end of the century, stationary steam and gasoline engines were used on a small number of farms to undertake tasks such as cutting oil-cake; but in the early twentieth century human muscle, oxen and horses still accounted for an overwhelming proportion of the power used on farms.

The rise of the tractor

The supremacy of the horse on the farm was in many countries surprisingly short-lived, for in 1892 the first commercial tractor was produced in the United States and similar experiments were undertaken in Britain, France and Germany. The tractor, driven of course by the internal combustion engine powered by petrol, was far more mobile than the steam engine and was much more easily manoeuvred. It was most rapidly adopted in the United States, where the most successful manufacturers – notably Ford – were found. Only 1000 were in use before the First World War, but the number had reached 1 million in 1930. The most radical change came in the 1940s, when labour shortages during the Second World War accelerated its adoption. By 1950 there were nearly 4 million tractors in use on farms in the United States. By the 1940s the spread of the tractor was such that most of the work capacity on American farms came from petrol-driven machines, electricity and other non-human and non-animal power (table 5.1).

In Western Europe the adoption of the tractor was slower than in the United States. The early tractors were not easy to use; they were often unstable, they had iron wheels, spares were difficult to obtain and there were few mechanics to repair them. British farmers used tractors to supplement their horses rather than to replace them. The decline of the horse before 1940 was due as much to the purchase of lorries and cars for use on farms as to the decline in their use in field work. In 1950, 85 per cent of the draught power used in European farming still came from horses and oxen, and it is only since then that the horse has been replaced by the tractor (figure 5.1). The rapid post-war adoption of the tractor has been speeded by great improvements: tractors now use diesel oil, have greater horse power and pneumatic tyres, and are more easily hitched to the implements they pull, whilst their engines can be used as a source of power for implements such as muck spreaders as well as being a source of traction. Above all, for much of the post-war period the low real cost of oil made their use economically viable.

Petrol-driven machines are not the only source of power on the modern farm. Dairy farms and broiler units rely upon electricity and a variety of tasks on the farmstead can be undertaken by machines powered by electricity. In irrigated areas and areas of drainage, electricity is an important source of power. Farms relied upon the spread of a national grid and this was most rapid in Western Europe. By the late 1930s virtually all the farms in the Netherlands and Switzerland were connected to an electrical supply, as were nine-tenths of those in Germany and Italy, four-fifths of those in Denmark and two-thirds of the farms in Sweden. In the United States, however, private electricity suppliers were reluctant to lay cables in sparsely populated rural areas, and in 1935 only 10 per cent of farms were connected. The government had to provide finance for the grid, and by 1950, 86 per cent of farms had an electricity supply.

The great growth of power available to farmers can be illustrated by the case of the United Kingdom. At the beginning of the twentieth century each worker in agriculture was supported by 1 horse-power of energy, mainly, of course, from horses. In 1939 this had risen to 3 hp, but by 1980 each worker was supported by 50 hp, an energy support greater than that in many manufacturing industries. By the 1960s, the number of tractors on British farms exceeded the number of workers.

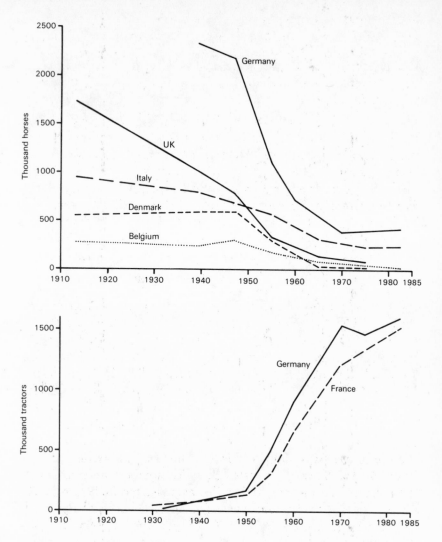

Figure 5.1 Changes in the numbers of horses and tractors in selected West European countries, 1910–85. (*Source*: P. Lamartine Yates, *Food Production in Western Europe*, London, 1940; Food and Agriculture Organization, *Production Yearbooks*, Rome.)

Mechanization

Although steam power was tried on farms in the nineteenth century, the replacement of animals as a source of traction has occurred only since the 1930s, and in many parts of Western Europe only since the 1950s. But the use of machines predates this; from the middle of the nineteenth century machines were drawn by horses or oxen. Not all parts of the production process were mechanized equally rapidly, however. Because cereals were the most important crop in most regions, the first efforts were directed towards reducing labour in their harvesting, and the machines designed for this purpose were relatively easily modified to cut grass. But fruit, tree crops, roots and livestock production were all more difficult to mechanize.

The cultivation of the seed-bed had been slowly improved over the centuries with better ploughs and harrows, and the introduction of the roller. The key innovation was the seed drill, which sowed seed in straight rows; it replaced hand broadcasting, but remarkably slowly. In Britain broadcasting was rare by the mid-nineteenth century, but in other parts of Europe it persisted. From the mid-eighteenth century, winnowing machines which separated the grain from the chaff were slowly adopted, and in the 1780s the threshing machine was invented. But the key innovation here was the reaper, which cut the grain in the field with moving scissor-like blades.

In the 1820s, Patrick Bell designed a reaper that worked, but in Britain there was little interest amongst farmers, for labour was abundant and cheap. In the United States, however, there was a great need for an effective reaper and Cyrus McCormick's invention in the 1830s was the machine that succeeded, for in the Mid-West labour was in short supply and farms were large; there was every incentive to adopt the reaper. It rapidly replaced the scythe (table 5.2). In Western Europe the replacement of the scythe was far slower, except in Britain where the labour force was declining after 1851, and where by the eve of the First World War, the reaper had replaced the scythe, except upon farms with very small acreages or on very steep slopes. In France and Germany most of the harvest was still got in with a scythe at the beginning of the twentieth century. In Australia, mechanization was at least as rapid

Table 5.2 Percentage of wheat harvested with the reaper

England and Wales		France	
1851	0%	1862	3.4%
1871	25%	1882	6.8%
1900	80%	1892	11.5%
1930	95%		
Germany		United States	
1882	3.6%	1850	negligible
1895	6.0%	1859	33–48%
		1870	80%

Sources: E. J. T. Collins, 'Labour supply and demand in European agriculture 1800–1880', in E. L. Jones and S. J. Woolf (eds), *Agrarian Change and Economic Development: The Historical Problems*, London, 1969, pp. 61–94; E. J. T. Collins, *Sickle to Combine: A Review of Harvest Techniques from 1800 to the Present Day*, Reading, 1969; P. A. David, 'The mechanization of reaping in the ante bellum mid-west', in H. Rosovsky (ed.), *Industrialisation in Two Systems*, London, 1966, pp. 3–39.

as in the United States; a reaper that cut the straw near the grain rather than near the ground – Ridley's stripper – was invented in the 1840s. By 1867, 89 per cent of South Australia's wheat was cut mechanically.

The basic reaper was later considerably improved. The early reaper simply cut the crop and deposited it in rows; men had to bind the straw into sheaves and put the sheaves in stooks to dry. But from the 1880s the reaper-binder accomplished both these tasks, although much labour was still needed in stooking and carting the grain. In Europe, grain was stored before threshing in ricks, whose construction relied upon the pitch fork; the elevator, another American invention, eased this task.

The separation of the head or grain from the straw had long been achieved by threshing – beating the harvested crop with a flail, two pieces of wood joined by leather. In Western Europe this was carried out in the slack time of the year, after Christmas and before spring cultivation, and for labourers employed by the day it was a vital source of income. It was, however, remarkably slow. The threshing machine, first used in Scotland in 1786, deprived labourers of winter wages, and in the early 1830s farm labourers in

England rioted in protest against its use. By 1850 only half the English wheat harvest was threshed by machine; but by the 1880s the flail had gone, and steam-driven machines were paramount. The threshing machine began to be used in the United States in the 1840s and spread rapidly, but elsewhere progress was slow. In Germany in the 1880s the flail was still used on one-third of the larger farms and most of the smaller; further east in Poland, two-thirds of all farms still used the flail in 1900.

The combine harvester

Even with the adoption of the reaper-binder, the threshing machine and the elevator, a great deal of labour was still used in harvesting the cereal crop. This was drastically reduced by the invention of the combine harvester, a machine that both cut and threshed the crop. Early experiments were made with combines in the American Mid-West in the 1840s; but its first important use was in California, where the machine was pulled either by great teams of horses or sometimes by steam engines. But before the First World War it was of little significance; there were only 270 manufactured in 1914. In the 1920s it began to be used in the wheat-producing regions of the Mid-West, and in 1929 a total of 36,957 combines were manufactured in the United States. Its progress was equally rapid in the other extensive grain-producing countries. In 1929, 30 per cent of the wheat in Argentina was combine-harvested and 15–16 per cent of that in Canada. The machine was introduced in Britain in 1927, but was little used there or in the rest of Europe before the Second World War. In the 1950s the United States had a substantial advantage in labour productivity over Western Europe, due to the earlier adoption of the tractor, the reaper-binder and the combine harvester. Even in England, which had adopted machines before most other parts of Europe, labour productivity lagged well behind the United States (table 5.3); in the 1950s it was only comparable to that in the United States between 1910 and 1930. In the 1950s labour needs in cereal production in Mediterranean countries were 26 times those in the United States, a difference roughly equivalent to that between traditional and modern agriculture. E. J. T. Collins has estimated the increase in labour productivity in wheat production in England between 1800 and 1965 as twenty-fold. The number of hours needed has continued to decline; a

Table 5.3 Number of man-hours needed to produce wheat from
1 hectare, 1950s

Traditional farming in:	
Mediterranean countries	260
Netherlands	130
Yugoslavia	91
Italy	60
Denmark	34
England	33
(United States, 1910–14	38)
United States, 1955–8	10
Great Plains	7

Source: Organization for Economic Co-operation and Development, *Problems of Manpower in Agriculture*, Paris, 1964, pp. 42, 49.

hectare of wheat required only one-third as much labour in the mid-1980s as it had done in 1965.

Roots and fruits

Cereal crops were the first to be harvested with machines; this was partly because of their great economic importance, but also because of the relative ease with which it could be done. Other crops presented greater difficulties. The root crops – sugar beet, potatoes and turnips – all needed to be both dug up and then lifted. The first attempts to mechanize potato picking occurred in Britain in the mid-nineteenth century, but only involved spinning the tuber from its ridge; the crop was picked by hand. Attempts to mechanize sugar beet began in Silesia in the 1860s, but it was not until the 1940s that successful harvesters were produced. The mechanization of sugar beet harvesting was then remarkably rapid in both the United States and England (table 5.4), as was that of the potato, once a machine that both dug and lifted had been designed. In both cases the mechanization of the crop has only been effective since the end of the Second World War. This has also been the case with a number of other crops. Eli Whitney's invention of the cotton gin in 1793 speeded the separation of the lint from the seed, but the

Table 5.4   Percentage of crop acreage mechanically harvested

Sugar beet, United States		Tomatoes, California	
1944	7	1965	1.5
1958	100	1968	95.0
Sugar beet, England and Wales		Cotton, United States	
1946	1	1949	10
1960	63	1969	96
Potatoes, United Kingdom			
1958	3		
1968	39		

Sources: W. D. Rasmussen, 'The mechanization of agriculture', *Scientific American*, 247 (1982), 49–61; R. K. Scott and A. Younger, 'Potato growing in a changing industry', *Outlook on Agriculture*, 7 (1972), 3–7; G. E. Jones, 'The diffusion of agricultural innovations,' in I. Burton and R. W. Kates (eds), *Readings in Resource Management and Conservation*, Chicago, 1970, pp. 475–92.

picking of cotton remained a hand operation although machines to do it were devised as early as the 1840s. The machine that finally accomplished the task was not patented until 1942, and mechanization was then very rapidly achieved (table 5.4). Fruit has always been difficult to harvest, for the individual fruits often ripen at different times, and are fragile and easily damaged by machines, whilst in the case of tree crops like apples, the fruit is inaccessible. The mechanization of harvesting has been partly dependent upon breeding new varieties. The tomato crop of the United States depended upon migrant workers until a variety was bred where each fruit ripened at the same time. Mechanical harvesting followed at a remarkable rate (table 5.4). Similarly, the mechanical harvesting of apples had to await the breeding of dwarf varieties. But much soft fruit and the more delicate vegetables remain hand-picked.

Livestock

In North America and Australasia most of the livestock were and are kept extensively; large numbers of animals feed upon natural and semi-natural vegetation and receive relatively little attention; livestock densities are low. In contrast, in Europe livestock have always received considerable attention from farmers. As mixed farming developed, part of the arable was set aside for growing fodder crops; later, cattle were housed and fed by hand, and oil-cake and other feeds were purchased to supplement hay and root crops. Cows were milked by hand. However, from the middle of the nineteenth century, dairying became a major form of specialization in Western Europe, the eastern United States and New Zealand, and attention was turned to the mechanization of production. The mechanization of hay-making was comparatively rapid, as a mower was in principle very similar to a reaper; a machine to turn grass whilst drying, the tedder, was also introduced in the later nineteenth century. Milking proved more difficult to master. A milking machine was patented in Scotland in 1895, but its adoption was slow. In 1939 four-fifths of the herds in Britain were still milked by hand; but in the post-war period, mechanization was rapid. It was equally rapid in the rest of Europe. In 1950 only 3 per cent of the cows in the countries later to form the EEC were milked by machine; by 1975 only 3 per cent were not.

Conclusions

The substitution of petrol and machines for men and animals has dramatically altered the nature of farming. The beginnings of modernization can be traced back to the first use of steam power on a farm in North Wales in 1798, but the first phase was still dependent upon animals – the first reapers, mowers and combines were drawn by horses, and indeed, outside the United States the horse or ox remained the prime source of energy on farms until after the end of the Second World War. The great industrial revival of Western Europe after 1945 drew men from the farms and led to the rapid mechanization of European agriculture, following the path long trodden in North America and Australasia, and, more slowly, in Britain.

6
The Growth of Markets

The increases in output and productivity over the last two centuries
have been due primarily to the adoption of new crops or techniques
on farms. The rate of this adoption, however, has been a function
of a great variety of factors, some of which are considered in this
and the following chapters. A prime stimulus to increased output
and productivity has been the growth of a market for agricultural
products. This chapter deals with the commercialization of agriculture: the use of money, the spread of market places, the growth of
population, changes in income and the demand for agricultural
produce, and the role of transport in increasing the size of the
market.

Subsistence farmers

It is often argued that a primary requirement for rapid agricultural
growth is that farmers be fully commercialized and respond to
changes in the price of the inputs they use and the price of the
goods that they sell. The commercial farmer is a businessman and
his main aim is to maximize profits. He has to judge which products will maximize profit and work out which is the cheapest way
to produce those goods. All his inputs are paid for; labour by
wages, land by rent and such inputs as fertilizers, seed and energy
are all bought from suppliers off the farm. Modern farming is a
matter of accountancy as much as practical skills. Commercial
farmers are in competition with each other and in the long run the
inept, the small – or the unlucky – will go under and the successful
will grow bigger.

Traditional farmers are said to be quite different in aims and
methods from the modern commercial farmers. Some economic
historians have argued that traditional farmers in the past were
different in economic behaviour from the modern farmer, and it is

the transition from tradition to modernity that must be traced. These are controversial issues: much has been written about the nature of peasants and the rise of individuality. A beginning can be made by defining the subsistence farmer.

Modern farmers do not try to provide all their own food. They specialize in a few products and buy their food from shops, and most of their produce is sold. In contrast, the subsistence farmer aims to produce as much of his family's needs as is possible; selling is a secondary consideration. In addition, the commercial farmer buys most of his inputs, whilst the subsistence farmer produces his own on the farm.

At some time, perhaps in the latter part of the first millennium, the great majority of the farmers of Western Europe were sub-sistence farmers. The rise of towns from the eleventh century stimulated sales, but whilst feudalism persisted little of the food produced left the farm, for the peasant consumed most of the produce on his own holding and raised food for his lord by labour-ing on the demesne. The spread of commercial farming – where farmers sell produce off the farm, and respond to changes in prices – is remarkably difficult to trace, for there are few statistics and there are difficulties in defining subsistence. Modern writers define subsistence in terms of the proportion of produce sold off the farm, but clearly there is a great range. A farmer who aims at producing only for his family needs, and never sells any produce, is unambi-guously a subsistence farmer. But what of the farmer who sells 5 per cent of his output? And at what point does the farmer pass from being a subsistence to a commercial farmer? Modern writers distinguish between the commercial farmer who sells over 50 per cent of output, and the semi-subsistence farmer who sells less than half, who aims first at self-sufficiency and only then at sales. The pure subsistence farmer, who neither sells nor buys at all, hardly exists in the modern world, and has been rare in Western Europe over the last eight hundred years. It should also be remembered that even modern commercial farmers do consume some of their own produce. In the 1960s it was estimated that 13–25 per cent of output was consumed on farms in Eastern Europe, 2–12 per cent in North-West Europe, and 7 per cent in the United States.

The term subsistence can be applied either to a farm or to a national economy, and the degree of subsistence can vary consider-ably according to location and size. Large farms are more likely to

be commercial than small, for a small-holding may well not produce enough to meet family needs, let alone a surplus for sale.
Thus in Switzerland at the beginning of this century those with
farms of less than 5 hectares consumed 42 per cent of their output,
but those with more than 30 hectares only 18 per cent. Farmers of
course need a market, and in a period of high transport costs those
near to towns are more likely to be commercial farmers than those
remote from non-agricultural populations. But the spread of commercialization in agriculture needed more than simply the reduction of transport costs. It needed money and markets.

Money and markets

The use of money in Europe began to be common in northern Italy
and the Low Countries in the twelfth century and spread slowly
elsewhere thereafter. In feudal society, peasants laboured on farms
in return for land, so wages were uncommon. With the decline of
serfdom, landlords began to pay wages for labour and peasants paid
rent in cash. Thus the spread of money accelerated, whilst conversely the wider use of money eroded feudalism. The rise of the
centralized nation-state, with its need for taxes, also increased the
use of money.

The term 'market' is used in a variety of ways. The first European markets – physical places where buyers and sellers meet – are
often attributed to the ninth century, although earlier examples
have been detected. Most of these early markets were coastal and
only later did inland markets serving local areas emerge. In England at least sixty markets are recorded in Domesday Book; all had
to be licensed by the king and were consequently an important
source of royal revenue. Markets were thus not necessarily competitive or ideally sited. There was a great expansion of markets in
England in the thirteenth century; by the end of the century there
were 1500.

This spread of markets was not confined to England; by 1500
Germany had 4000 market towns. Thereafter the numbers in
England declined; as royal power waned, markets became more
competitive and some increased in size, others disappeared.
Three-quarters of those founded in England between 1200 and
1349 had gone by the seventeenth century. The more successful

markets freed themselves from royal or baronial control at an early date, notably in northern Italy and the Low Countries.

At least as early as the twelfth century, ordinary peasants were taking produce to market, although not all produce was marketed in this way. Direct sales were common in England, notably of wool and grain. But by the later Middle Ages, markets and money existed in sufficient quantities to allow the commercialization of agriculture in all but the remoter parts of Western Europe. Although there was long-distance trade in the more valuable agricultural commodities – grain, wine and wool – most markets served only local areas. The next stage in the spread of markets was the formation of a hierarchy, or system of markets, whereby one market set the price for a surrounding number of smaller markets. This was followed by the establishment of regional markets; in England the county towns served this purpose. England and France would then be served by a number of regional systems, each with its own price. Later, metropolitan markets emerged. In England and France this occurred in the sixteenth century, when London and Paris became the dominant markets because of their great size and wealth and were provisioned by large tributary areas, so that gradually a uniform price for the whole country emerged. By the eighteenth century, regional prices were disappearing in England and the country was one great market area, but France's greater size meant that regional price differences persisted into the nineteenth century.

There had been international trade in agricultural products before the sixteenth century, but it was very limited; indeed, even today, only one-twelfth of the world's agricultural output crosses national boundaries, and in the eighteenth century less than 1 per cent of European grain production did so. But from the sixteenth century international trade slowly increased and the beginnings of an international market became apparent. Amsterdam became the centre of a trade in grain; it was grown on the estates of Poland and East Germany, shipped down rivers to the Baltic and thence to the Low Countries. Part of this was reshipped to Mediterranean states. European settlement in the Americas led to the export of high-value products such as tobacco from Virginia and sugar from the West Indies and Brazil, whilst the long-established overland trade in spices from India and South-East Asia became maritime. By the early nineteenth century, Western Europe was a market for grain from the United States, Eastern Europe and Russia. But a true world market, with North-West Europe at its centre, had to await increases in the size of ships, a fall in the cost of overland and ocean freight rates, and the telegraph and cable that could create world prices. By the late nineteenth century, meat, butter, hides, wool, and grain flowed from Australia, Argentina, North America and Russia to Western Europe; but even then only a small part of output entered into international trade, and the greater part of world output was still consumed upon farms.

The spread of commercialization

Neither the spread of money nor the growth of markets gives an adequate measure of the spread of commercialization. As long as a large proportion of the population of a country was engaged in agriculture and non-agricultural populations were a minority, it was inevitable that a majority of the food produced would be consumed upon farms and not marketed. Thus in the early nineteenth century the United States was still an agrarian economy. In 1820 only 25 per cent of output was sold off the farm, and the proportion did not exceed 50 per cent until the 1860s; in Norway in 1845, 80 per cent of the total population were engaged in a subsistence economy. As already noted, the size of farm influenced the amount marketed. Thus in East Germany in 1800, peasants on small farms marketed only 20 per cent of their output, for they had first to produce their own needs; but their lords, with much larger acreages, marketed over half their grain output. By the mid-nineteenth century a higher proportion of agricultural output was being sold off the farm in Western Europe, but further east most produce was still mainly for subsistence purposes. In 1850, only 15 per cent of Russian grain left the farms, 90 per cent of this accounted for by nobles from their large estates. This difference between Western and Eastern Europe persisted into the twentieth century: in the 1930s only half Romania's food output was sold off farms, and in the remoter parts of Eastern Europe such as Croatia or Transylvania, no more than a quarter or a third of the food produced was sent to markets.

Tracing the decline of subsistence farming is difficult, for there are few reliable statistics. Clearly many – perhaps a majority – of farmers before the later nineteenth century were semi-subsistence;

that is, they aimed at providing family needs but also sold to obtain cash to provide those items that they could not produce on the farm. Thus in the late eighteenth century some farmers on the east coast of the United States were selling grain for export to Western Europe, but their main concern was still the provision of family needs. Indeed, it was not until after the Civil War that more than half of total output was being sold off the farm, although by then the United States was a major exporter of wheat and cotton, and was also provisioning its rapidly growing cities.

The consequences of commercialization

As farmers were drawn more and more into the production of goods for sale, there were a number of consequences. First, farmers became increasingly influenced by the prices of agricultural products. The long-term trend in grain prices determined the periods of expanding output, when extra land was brought into cultivation; when grain prices were low, expansion halted, and land was often abandoned. In most periods of falling grain prices, the prices of livestock and industrial crops such as flax or chicory fell less, and farmers turned to these products. Second, the traditional farmer relied primarily upon family labour and consumed most of his output; he was not greatly influenced by prices either of product or input. But once drawn into commercial farming, prices began to determine his behaviour, and enabled him to become more efficient. Without the guide of prices it was difficult for him to see how to economize, or whether to exploit his labour force, add land or use more horse-power. Third, the commercialization of farming encouraged specialization, and specialization increases efficiency and productivity. Farmers concentrated upon one or two products, and regions specialized in those products in which they had a comparative advantage; specialization, however, also made farmers more vulnerable to price declines.

The growth of the market for farm produce

Modern economists often debate whether economic growth is prompted by increases in supply, which creates its own market; or whether demand creates the technological changes which lead to increases in supply. Certainly in the long run demand for agricultural produce seems to be of great importance in causing farmers to expand output and to change the type of goods they make available. Changes in demand over time result from three principal factors: the increase – or decrease – in population; the changing incomes of consumers; and the needs of industry. Population growth has been touched upon already. The periods of more rapid population growth, 1100–1320, 1480–1640 and 1750 to the 1820s, saw supply fail to meet demand and so prices rose, stimulating further production. Population growth acted upon commercial farmers through the price mechanism, but also influenced subsistence farmers who sought to meet the needs of larger families by working harder or clearing new land.

One measure of the growth of the market for farmers is total population; in Western Europe there was growth in the sixteenth century, decline in the later seventeenth century, substantial growth in the eighteenth century and dramatic increase in the nineteenth century (table 6.1). But the market for sales off the farm is not accurately measured by total population growth. The ratio between farmers and non-farmers is the best index, but such figures are not available. However, estimates of the population in places where it was over 10,000, and of the total population, are available. The rate of increase of the urban population (table 6.1c) grew more rapidly in the sixteenth than the seventeenth century, and accelerated in the second half of the eighteenth century; after 1800 the urban population doubled in each half century. But it must be remembered that the non-urban population was growing as well until the late nineteenth century (figure 3.2), and the ratio between the urban and non-urban population may be a better guide to the growth of the market (table 6.1B). Although this confirms the importance of the sixteenth century, the growth of the number of non-farmers to farmers was comparatively slow in the seventeenth and eighteenth centuries (table 6.1D), and it is the period after 1800 which has seen explosive growth of the market.

The rapid rise of the urban market in the nineteenth century had considerable consequences for the farmers of Western Europe. Because the ratio of the non-agricultural to the agricultural population increased, agricultural output and productivity also had to increase; but towards the end of the nineteenth century, farmers in

Table 6.1 The urban and rural populations of Western Europe, 1500–1940 (millions)

	1500	1550	1600	1650	1700	1750	1800	1850	1890	1940
Urban	3.4	4.3	5.8	6.4	7.3	8.6	12.2	28.2	62.1	162.0
Rural	58.2	59.3	64.5	61.4	66.7	76.2	98.3	129.9	141.6	105.0
Total	61.6	63.6	70.3	67.5	74.0	84.8	110.5	158.1	203.7	267.0
A	5.5	6.8	8.3	9.0	9.8	10.1	11.1	17.8	30.5	60.6
B	5.8	7.0	9.0	10.0	11.0	11.0	12.0	22.0	44.0	154.0

	1500–50	1550–1600	1600–50	1650–1700	1700–50	1750–1800	1800–50	1850–1900	1890–1940
C	26.4	34.8	10.3	14.0	17.8	49.3	131.1	120.2	160.8
D	21.0	29.0	11.0	10.0	0.0	9.0	83.0	100.0	250.0

A: Number of people in places of more than 10,000 as a percentage of the total population.
B: Number of persons in places of more than 10,000 to every 100 of the non-urban population.
C: Percentage increase in the number in places of more than 10,000.
D: Percentage increase in the ratio B.

Source: J. De Vries, *European Urbanization 1600–1800*, London, 1984; A. Weber, *The Growth of Cities in the Nineteenth Century*, New York, 1899; United Nations, *Demographic Yearbook 1952*, New York, 1953.

Western Europe were unable to provide an adequate food supply, and Western Europe hecame dependent upon the import of food and animal feeds from overseas, and remained so until the 1960s.

Diet, income and demand

Although population change is a major element in the demand for agricultural products, it is not the only factor. The ability of the consumer to pay for food is vital, and changes in incomes, particularly since 1850, have influenced the type of food purchased, which in turn has affected the type of farming practised.

Little is known about incomes in pre-industrial Europe, or of food consumption levels. The real incomes of the great majority of the population, whether rural or urban, were low. There is some evidence that real wages were at a peak in the early fifteenth century, after a long period of declining population due to outbreaks of bubonic plague, and declined thereafter, and did not reach this level again until the second half of the nineteenth century. Most people spent a high proportion of their low incomes on food. A skilled worker in Amsterdam in the late sixteenth century spent 70 per cent of his wages on food; 200 years later, miners in Durham spent the same proportion. The actual expenditure was small; families tried to maximize the number of calories per unit of money they spent. The cheapest source of energy before the eighteenth century was the cereal crop. Wheat and rye gave flour that could be made into bread, oats could be consumed as oatcakes or porridge, and even barley, grown for malt to make beer, was used to produce a flour. Cereals were a cheap source of calories, but if eaten in sufficient quantities provided enough protein as well.

Livestock products – meat, milk, cheese and eggs – were eaten; they all provide protein in concentrated form as well as energy. But livestock products were and are more expensive per calorie than cereals, because livestock production requires more land than wheat or barley to produce a calorie. Cereals are consumed directly by man, whereas livestock graze grass or feed upon grains, and so less of the original energy is available to man. It takes approximately five to six times as much land to provide one calorie of energy from livestock products as it does one calorie of energy from crops. Crops produce not only more calories per hectare than livestock

Table 6.2 Output of calories and protein per hectare and per man-hour
in Britain in the early twentieth century

	Calories (MK calories)		Protein (kg)	
	Output per hectare	Output per 100 man-hours	Output per hectare	Output per 100 man-hours
Wheaten flour	2.0	9.3	67	280
Potatoes	5.7	3.4	133	77
Dairy products	0.5	0.7	25	27
Beef	0.25	0.3	10	18

Source: P. Mumford, 'The cost of nutrients in the first half of the twentieth century', in D. J. Oddy and D. S. Miller (eds), *Diet and Health in Modern Britain*, London, 1985, p. 298.

(table 6.2), but more protein per hectare: crop production of both calories and protein is also more efficient per man-hour worked.

European farmers had a limited range of food crops in the medieval and early modern period: most of them had been acquired from South-West Asia. The discovery of the Americas led to the exchange of plants and animals between the two continents. Europe acquired turkeys, tobacco, tomatoes and maize, but most importantly, potatoes. The potato gave a higher yield of calories per hectare than cereals (table 6.2) and was widely adopted as a food crop from the late eighteenth century.

There is little reliable evidence on food consumption in Western Europe before the nineteenth century, but what fragmentary data there is suggests that for the majority of the population the calorie intake was similar to that in many of the poorer developing countries today, with national averages of about 2000 calories *per caput* per day. Many of the population must have suffered from deficiency diseases due to the lack of protein, vitamin C and other nutrients. Energy intakes were low, and low at a time when most jobs required heavy manual labour.

The industrial revolution slowly increased the incomes of most of the population of Western Europe, although there is much debate as to when the benefits reached the mass of the population. It seems agreed, however, that real incomes rose in Western Europe after 1850, and for some sectors of the population were rising before then. This had important effects on food consumption. At first, the poor who had an increase in income simply ate more of

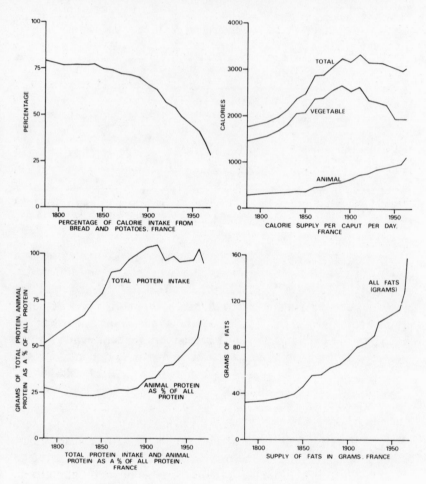

Figure 6.1 Changes in the French diet, 1790–1960. (*Source*: J. C. Toutain, *La Consommation alimentaire en France de 1789 à 1964*, Paris, 1971.)

the cheap staples such as cereals and potatoes. Later they shifted from inferior cereals to the preferred cereal. In Western Europe this led to the primacy of wheat, as rye and oats were eaten less.

In the nineteenth century, calorie consumption *per capita* increased in Western Europe as the population became better off (figure 6.1). But the composition of the diet did not initially change: in France in 1870, 70 per cent of all calories were still derived from cereals and potatoes and most of the protein intake came from vegetable products. But from the end of the nineteenth century the West European diet began to change profoundly. Higher incomes allowed more meat, more milk, more eggs and more cheese to be purchased. In addition, the consumption of fruit and fresh vegetables increased. More luxury products were consumed. French and German sugar consumption trebled in the last twenty years of the nineteenth century and tea, chocolate and coffee were imported from the tropics and subtropics. By the beginning of this century, calorie consumption *per capita* had reached a peak: it was the composition of the diet that now changed, with increasing proportions of calorie and protein intake coming from animal foods; in some countries the absolute consumption of the old staples, bread and potatoes, began to decline (figure 6.1).

The growth of urban populations and incomes in the nineteenth century provided a growing market not only for the industrializing countries of Western Europe, but for North America, Australasia and temperate South America. It was this, of course, that stimulated the great expansion in the cultivated area overseas (see above, pp. 17–20). The growth of incomes combined with the import of extensively produced grains, meat and wool prompted major changes in the farming of Western Europe. The importance of livestock in the agrarian economies of all these countries increased substantially. In Denmark, cheap grain was imported to feed cows and pigs, and butter and bacon were exported to the prosperous industrial populations of Britain and Germany. British farmers slowly switched from their traditional mixed farms to more specialized enterprises, particularly to dairying and horticulture; these two accounted for only one-fifth of the value of British agricultural output in the 1860s, but two-fifths by 1951. By the 1950s farmers in Western Europe faced a new problem: the demand for agricultural produce, which had been increasing at a remarkable rate for some two hundred years, began to slow down. There were two reasons: population growth slowed in the 1930s, and the rates of increase since then have been low; more importantly, incomes *per capita* in Western Europe, North America and Australasia since 1945 have reached remarkably high levels, so while until the 1930s malnutrition was still common amongst parts of the West European population, and any increases in income were spent on extra food, in the immediate post-war period, rising real incomes did not lead to any great increase in expenditure upon food, even on the more expensive foodstuffs. The market was virtually saturated, although people were prepared to spend more on the processing of food and convenience foods. For some foods in Britain, increases in income in the 1980s brought a decline in consumption, and for many others increases were very small. Adam Smith put it more elegantly: 'The desire of food is limited in every man by the narrow capacity of the human stomach; but the desire of the conveniences and ornaments of building, dress, equipage, and household furniture, seems to have no limit or certain boundary.'

The industrial revolution and raw materials

The great growth of population and incomes in the late eighteenth and nineteenth centuries increased the demand for food. The rise of factory production, population and incomes also stimulated the demand for agricultural products that could by used in industry, and this had an impact upon farmers in Europe and especially in the European settlements overseas. Wool had always been an important product in Western Europe, although sheep were kept mainly in upland areas; only in Britain were sheep integrated into lowland mixed farming. The growth of the textile industries led to an increase in the number of sheep, but it was insufficient to meet demand, and extensive sheep production was established in the sparsely settled hinterlands of Australia, New Zealand, South Africa and Patagonia. The wool of these sheep was generally of finer quality than that of those kept in Europe, which were increasingly bred for mutton and so produced a poorer wool. The high unit value of wool allowed it to be shipped the considerable distance to the markets, whilst the extensive methods of production meant it was cheaper than European wool. In the 1870s European wool production began a long decline.

The other fibre for which demand increased was cotton. In the eighteenth century, cotton had been imported in small amounts into Western Europe from the Mediterranean and later from the West Indies. The technical advances in the British cotton textile industry in the second half of the eighteenth century led to a growth in demand for cotton, which was met by an expansion of the cotton-growing area in the United States. At first, cotton was only grown in the southern Atlantic states, but it expanded westwards and was being grown in Texas by the mid-nineteenth century. The growth of industry in Europe prompted demand for other raw materials too, such as vegetable oils and rubber, but these were most easily produced in the tropics.

Agricultural products, transport and the market

Even before improvements in transport took place, some agricultural products did move considerable distances; but the distance over which products could be moved profitably varied greatly. Cattle and sheep, and to a lesser extent pigs, could be driven, although they lost weight and ideally needed fattening up near market. In Britain, London has long been the major market for meat. Cattle were often reared in the uplands; Welsh cattle were being driven to London as early as the thirteenth century, whilst in the seventeenth century, cattle reared in Ireland and Scotland were driven to pastures near London to be prepared for market. As early as the sixteenth century the larger cities of Western Europe, particularly those in the Low Countries, imported cattle reared in Eastern Europe and fattened them for market. In the United States in the nineteenth century, cattle were bred and reared in Texas, then driven north to railheads; they were then taken to the Corn Belt to be fattened on maize for the meat packers.

Other agricultural products had of course to be transported to market. There were great variations in the distance which crops could be economically moved; mid-nineteenth century Germany offers some examples (figure 6.2). Products with a very high value per unit weight could be moved long distances; wool and sugar are obvious examples. Some low-value products could be processed on the farm, and the higher-value product transported greater distances: thus grain and potatoes could be converted into alcohol, milk into cheese and butter. Before the invention of refrigeration, perishable goods had to be produced near the market; consequently most great cities had a zone of milk, fruit and vegetable production on their fringes, and indeed many still do. Products with a very low value per unit weight also had to be produced near the market, so that potatoes, sugar beet and fodder roots were rarely transported any great distance (figure 6.2).

Not surprisingly, then, crops and livestock could be found in

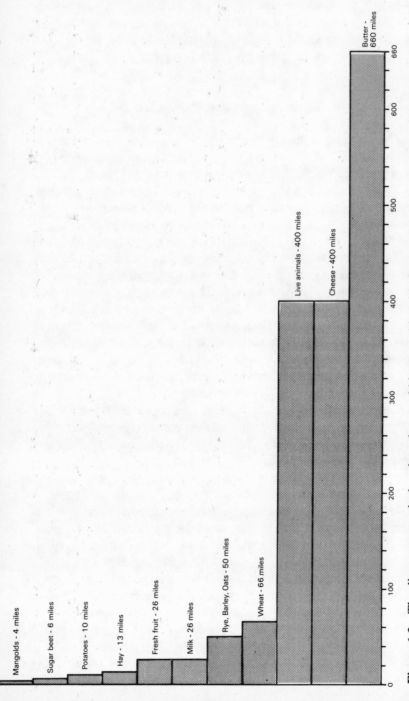

Figure 6.2 The distance an agricultural product could be moved in mid-nineteenth-century Germany before cost of transport equalled value. (*Source:* E. T. Benedict, H. H. Stoppler and M. R. Nemedoct (eds), *Theodore Brinkmann's Economics of the Farm Business*, Berkeley, CA, 1935).

Mangolds - 4 miles
Sugar beet - 6 miles
Potatoes - 10 miles
Hay - 13 miles
Fresh fruit - 26 miles
Milk - 26 miles
Rye, Barley, Oats - 50 miles
Wheat - 66 miles
Live animals - 400 miles
Cheese - 400 miles
Butter - 660 miles

zones around the great cities of the pre-industrial world. Nearby there was fresh milk, fresh vegetables, hay for horses in the city; horse dung could be bought by these farmers to increase yields. Beyond this intensive zone cereals and industrial crops were grown in rotation, without fallow, whilst beyond was the great zone of open-field farming, where cereals and fallow alternated. The rearing of livestock took place at some distance from the cities.

This zonation was described by the German economist J. H. von Thünen in 1826; he wrote at a time when carts hauled by oxen were still the main means of transport. But in the nineteenth century, as the urban demand for food increased, and as transport costs fell, so the intensive practices found near the cities spread outwards and the less intensive, such as livestock rearing, were pushed to the peripheries. Indeed, the more extensive farming systems took root in the New World and Australia, where cheap land and mechanization allowed the extensive production of meat, wheat and wool that could supply Western Europe's cities, whilst Western European farming from the 1880s became progressively more intensive.

Transport and agricultural change

Much of the economic change of the last two hundred years has been dependent upon a reduction in the cost of movement of raw materials, products and people. Both rural–urban migration and migration overseas took place before the nineteenth century, but the railway and the steamship reduced the cost of movement and so accelerated the flow of people. Again, the movement of raw materials for industry and the distribution of manufactured goods was made cheaper, although the proximity of raw materials remained important for the location of industry. Similarly, agricultural growth was stimulated by the falling real cost of moving both inputs and products. Better transport increased the size of the market for farmers, made it possible to provision the very large cities that emerged in the nineteenth century, and cheapened the movement of inputs to farms. Falling transport costs made it possible for farmers to buy coal for steam threshers, for large quantities of oil-cake and other feedstuffs to be moved, and for fertilizers such as guano or Chile saltpetre to be imported from South America.

The introduction of the railway and the steamship in the second half of the nineteenth century had a considerable effect on the price of transport, but there had already been important reductions in the cost of moving agricultural goods. The bulk of internal movement took place overland. In most of Europe roads were in a very poor condition until the seventeenth century and high speeds were impossible, making the marketing of perishable commodities like fresh milk difficult. Before the eighteenth century, much internal freight was carried by pack horses; but because they could carry only small amounts, costs were high. Larger quantities could be hauled in two-wheeled wagons, only replaced by four wheels in the seventeenth century. The substitution of horses for oxen substantially reduced costs; in France in the eighteenth and nineteenth centuries haulage by oxen was twice as expensive as by horse – but in most of Western Europe oxen were not replaced by horses until the nineteenth century. Roads began to be improved by turnpike trusts in England in the seventeenth century, and in the early nineteenth century MacAdam's improved surfacing methods allowed larger, faster carts and the replacement of oxen by horses. There is no doubt that the cost of overland movement was falling before the spread of the railway. In France, for example, road transport costs fell between 30 per cent and 50 per cent between 1810 and 1850.

Until the nineteenth century transport by water was cheaper than transport over land, so coastal shipping and rivers were important ways of moving agricultural produce, particularly grain. The relative cost of land and water transport has been variously estimated. One authority suggests that land costs were 4–5 times those of rivers in the seventeenth century, another merely three times. In any case, the difference was substantial, although the number of navigable rivers was limited. In England in 1660 only 1095 km of rivers were navigable, but this had risen to 1856 km by 1720. Canals began to be an important means of communication in the eighteenth and early nineteenth centuries.

Oceanic freight rates were also falling before the age of steam. The frequency of war kept them high until 1815; thereafter there was a continuous decline, even though steam did not supplant sail for the movement of bulk commodities until the 1880s. Shipping began to be better organized, with shorter periods idle in ports, and there was greater knowledge of winds and currents.

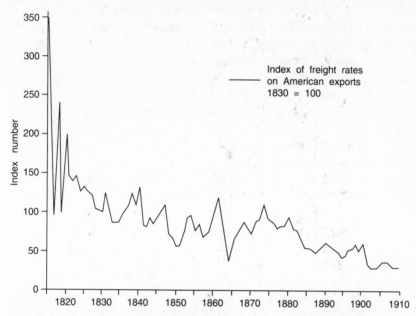

Figure 6.3 Index of oceanic freight rates on American exports (1830 = 100). (*Source*: J. R. Peet, 'The spatial expansion of commercial agriculture in the nineteenth century: a von Thünen interpretation', *Economic Geography*, 45, 1969, 283–301.)

The spread of the railway and the steamship in the second half of the nineteenth century thus accelerated a long-term downward trend in the real cost of moving agricultural produce. Some of the gains were substantial. In Western Europe in the second half of the nineteenth century it was 3–4 times more expensive to move goods by road than by rail; not surprisingly, as early as 1860 half the wheat and flour in France went by train; the railway accounted for nearly all the movement of fertilizer by 1900; and by 1914, 70 per cent of all freight in the country travelled by rail. The railway reduced freight costs everywhere it spread; in 1873 it cost 34 cents to send a bushel of wheat from Chicago to New York, by 1905 only 8 cents. The fall in oceanic freight rates continued in the second half of the nineteenth century (figure 6.3); in 1873 the freight on a bushel of wheat from New York to Liverpool was 21 cents, in 1901, 3 cents. Over the same period freight rates on wool from Australia to England were halved.

The late nineteenth century saw the introduction of refrigeration, an important change, for it allowed the transport of meat and dairy products over long distances and of meat rather than live cattle. Ice-boxes were first used on American railways in the 1860s, and refrigeration cars in the 1880s. Equally significant was the installation of refrigeration on ships; the first chilled beef reached England from New York in 1875, and France from Buenos Aires in 1877. Frozen meat was sent from Australia to London in 1879, and from New Zealand three years later. By the 1890s, butter from New Zealand was reaching London; in 1901 bananas arrived from Jamaica.

The twentieth century has seen further improvements in transport, and the cost of transport as a proportion of the sale price has continued to fall. The most striking feature has been the reappearance of road transport as the main overland carrier of agricultural products. Initially lorries were only used to connect farms with railheads, but in the post-war period the lorry has supplanted the railway, partly because of its greater flexibility. Remote areas, beyond the railway, have been drawn into the economy.

Conclusions

Until the nineteenth century, economic and demographic changes in Western Europe were slow. The growth of population stimulated agricultural output and the rise of great cities provided an increased market. But it was the nineteenth century that saw an unparalleled expansion of the market, as urbanization greatly increased the number of non-farmers to be fed by each farmer. The widening of the market was made possible by the falling real cost of transport.

7

Serfs, Tenants and Villagers

In the 1950s many who wrote about the agricultural problems of the developing world thought that a major obstacle to increasing output and productivity was the lack of incentive for the farmer, and that a principal cause of this was the landownership system prevailing in many countries, where landlords had too much power, took too much of the farmers' output in excessive rents, evicted tenants at will, did little to improve the productive capacity of farms, and made no attempt to provide land for a rapidly growing population.

Thirty years later less stress is placed upon the central role of land reform as a means of 'getting agriculture going' in the developing countries, partly because of the great difficulties of persuading governments to implement reform – particularly in Latin America – and partly because land reform, where it has occurred, has not always led to great improvements in efficiency. Nor has there been any unanimity as to what should replace landlordism. Collectivization has not been a success in Russia, Eastern Europe or China; on the other hand, the creation of independent occupier-owners – in Iran or India for example – has not necessarily led to better farming, for other changes such as improved transport or easier credit are often needed to spur improvement.

Not surprisingly, the history of landownership has attracted great attention. The ownership of land was the source of economic and political power in traditional society and indeed still persists. H. H. Asquith, at the beginning of the twentieth century, was the first British prime minister not to own land. Given the great importance of land, its unequal distribution, and particularly its concentration in relatively few hands, has been a matter of great concern. Agricultural historians have been interested in the equity of land distribution, and the effect of land ownership upon productivity. It has been generally argued that ideally land is owned by the man who works it; under these circumstances the farmer is not burdened by rent payments or labour services and is not constrained by a landlord in the way he manages his farm; his tenure is secure and he cannot be evicted; and the benefits of an investment or the technological improvements he makes accrue to him or his descendants. Where the farmer does not own the land, circumstances may be – and often have been – highly adverse to good farming, and agricultural progress is inhibited. However, not all tenancy systems are necessarily bad; tenants can be protected by law against excessive rent increases or eviction, and compensated for improvements on leaving the farm. Indeed, where, as in England from the early eighteenth century, both tenant and landlord invested in improvements, the landlord/tenant system had advantages.

The traditional farmer in Europe was slowly freed from the disadvantages of landlordism, first by the decline of feudalism, and in the nineteenth and twentieth centuries by government policies that encouraged the growth of owner-occupying; but the farmer's behaviour, and particularly his propensity to adopt innovations, was often constrained by the prevailing system of collective village farming; in this chapter, the decline of tenancy and the village collective are described.

Feudalism

In the eleventh and twelfth centuries feudalism spread rapidly over most of lowland Western Europe, but developed only weakly in Eastern Europe. Agricultural land was subjected to seigniors in the form of manors, which were often scattered across a wide area. This land was divided into two parts: the demesne, which provided the seignior's own needs, and the remainder, which was divided among the serfs. In return for this land the serf had to work for several days each week on the demesne. The serf had other obligations to the lord, which varied greatly in time and place; these included *banalitiés* such as using the lord's mill to grind corn, paying tolls, undertaking non-agricultural labour – on maintaining roads, for example – and paying fines on death, births and marriage. Serfs were not allowed to leave the manor, nor usually were their children, who provided the next generation of serfs. In return the lord provided military protection, law and administration.

Serfdom began a long decline in the thirteenth century with the wider use of money and the rise of towns. Slowly the prerogatives of the seigniors were eroded. By the sixteenth century emerging nation-states with strong centralized governments were providing law, protection and administration. The peasant's status was also changing; as W. Slicher van Bath has written, 'In Western Europe, to the west of the river Elbe, the manorial system, feudal relations between lords and peasants, and medieval villeinage disappeared between the twelfth and sixteenth centuries.'

By 1500 most peasants were free to move from their village, free to sell the land they occupied – although normally paying a fine to the lord – and free to decide who would inherit their holding. The obligation to provide labour on the demesne had declined after the fourteenth century, to be replaced by cash payments, which were not, however, until the eighteenth century or later, economic rents.

By the eighteenth century a number of different forms of tenure had evolved from the feudal period. In parts of Scandinavia, Britain, West Germany and the Low Countries, there were free peasant proprietors, who had no rent to pay or other obligations to a lord. They were however, few in number, and in England had been in decline for two centuries or more. A second form was hereditary tenure, where the peasant had the right to will the land and could sell it, but only with the lord's permission. The lord could evict and could also control the way farming was carried out. With the formal ending of serfdom in the late eighteenth and early nineteenth centuries, these farmers became occupier-owners in France, the Low Countries and south-west Germany. A third form of tenure was leasehold; if for life, or for several lives, it gave the tenant security of tenure and the incentive to make long-term improvements; but where it was for a short period the tenant had no protection against eviction at the end of the lease, nor against sharp increases in rent when the lease was renewed. Finally, there was share-cropping, particularly important in Italy, Spain and southern France. Under this system the landlord provided the land and often much of the working capital, the tenant the labour and some working capital; the output was shared between tenant and landlord in a predetermined proportion.

Whilst serfdom had disappeared from Western Europe by the sixteenth century, it had then only just taken root east of the Elbe, and it spread over much of Poland, East Germany, Hungary, the

Balkans and Russia in far more onerous forms than had existed in the West. Hence in the period of peasant emancipation in the eighteenth century the acts that ended the legal status of serfdom had little practical consequence in the West, except to end or restrict the payment of *banalitiés*, whereas in the East they ended a repressive system of land-holding that often included personal bondage. Legislation to emancipate the peasant began in Savoy in 1771 and was soon followed by reforms in Baden, Denmark and Switzerland. In France the Revolution ended *banalitiés* without greatly increasing peasant ownership of land. By 1850, emancipation had taken place everywhere except in Hungary, Romania and Russia; the latter ended serfdom in 1864.

Whilst serfdom existed it placed an intolerable burden upon the farm family; little income was left for saving and subsequent investment in farm improvement. In Brandenburg in the early fourteenth century half the peasant's harvest went to the seignior. Five centuries later, in villages in Brunswick, between one-third and one-half of the harvest was taken. As late at the eighteenth century the *banalitiés* imposed in southern France accounted for 10 per cent of peasant gross income, and money rent, taxes and tithe accounted for half of gross income. The *taille*, the main tax, was not paid by nobles or some of the urban middle classes, and so fell mainly upon the peasantry.

The final emancipations of the late eighteenth century removed many injustices, but for the most part in Western Europe only confirmed long-established forms of land tenure. In the East, however, peasants lost land as part of the indemnification of seigniors for their loss of services. Thus in east Germany and Hungary larger estates emerged in the nineteenth century, run by their owners and worked by landless labourers. The end of serfdom did not make all West European farmers into occupier-owners. There are few reliable statistics on the relative prevalence of tenancy and occupier-owning before the late nineteenth century; but then tenancy still persisted (table 7.1). In the Low Countries rich urban dwellers had bought land in the Middle Ages, and so two-thirds of all farmers in Belgium, and nearly half in the Netherlands and Denmark, were tenants; whilst in France, particularly northern France, tenants were numerous: about half the area was farmed by tenants, although three-quarters of all farmers were occupier-owners. Britain was the nation of tenants *par excellence*; occupier-owners were few by the early eighteenth century.

Table 7.1 Percentage of farmers and farmland owner-operated

		Numbers	Area
England and Wales	1910	13	12
	1961	56	49
Ireland	1929	–	98
Norway	1949	91	88
Denmark	1850	50	–
	1885	89	–
	1930	95	–
	1949	96	97
Netherlands	1888	58	–
	1910	51	–
	1930	56	–
	1959	55	48
Belgium	1846	35	–
	1880	32	–
	1925	43	41
	1930	48	–
	1959	45	32
France	1882	74	–
	1892	70	53
	1929	75	60
	1955	72	57
Germany	1933	90	–
	1966	89	81
Germany	1907	–	86
Switzerland	1929	83	74

Source: F. Dovring, *Land and Labour in Europe in the Twentieth Century*, The Hague, 1965, pp. 168–9; P. Lamartine Yates, *Food Production in Western Europe*, London, 1940.

There is no evidence that the tenant farmers in northern France, England or the Low Countries were, in the eighteenth and nineteenth centuries, less efficient than the occupier-owners. They had little legal protection, and relied upon the goodwill of landlords. Only in the late nineteenth century was there legislation to guarantee compensation for unexhausted improvements when a tenant left a farm. But security of tenure in law was not obtained in England until 1941, in the Netherlands until 1937 and in France until 1947.

From the middle of the nineteenth century public opinion and government policy began to favour the conversion of tenancies into occupier-ownerships; this was achieved in Denmark between 1850 and 1885, and in Ireland between the 1880s and 1920. In Britain the 1920s and the post-1945 period saw a dramatic decline in tenancy. In Norway, West Germany and Switzerland the peasant proprietor had become dominant much earlier, and there has been little change in this century.

The village community

During the Middle Ages most Europeans lived in villages; farms and other buildings were grouped together at a central point in the parish or commune, and there were few isolated farmsteads. Admittedly, some areas, such as Ireland and the west of Britain, Norway and parts of Germany, were characterized by more dispersed settlements with hamlets and solitary dwelling houses, but the village predominated in lowland Britain, northern France and eastwards along the north European plain into Russia. Most of these villages had the open-field system of farming; although there were many variations of this pattern, there were certain common features.

First, the farmhouses were in the village which lay at the centre of between two and seven very large arable fields; in the Danish village of Østerstillinge, for example, there were three such fields (figure 7.1). Each field was divided into what in England were called furlongs or shots, in Germany *Gewanne*, and in Denmark *aase*. The blocks were in turn divided into strips, which though varying in size and shape, were predominantly long and narrow, typically 220 yards long by 22 yards (200 × 20 metres) wide. Neither these strips nor the furlongs were enclosed by hedges or walls, although the great fields might be separated from each other by wattle fences. Each farm consisted of a number of these strips, which however were not contiguous; rather they were intermingled with those of other farmers, and most farms had strips in each of the great fields, as were those of Niels Lund in Østerstillinge (figure 7.1).

There is no entirely satisfactory explanation for this intermixture. It may simply have been due to the subdivision of farms

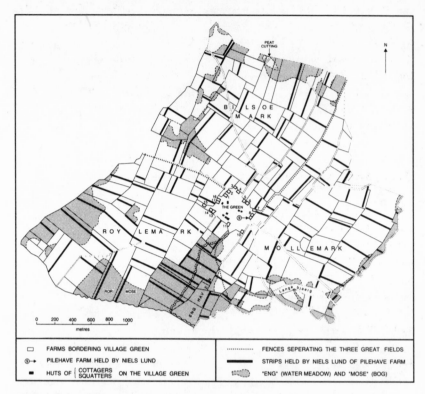

Figure 7.1 The township of Østerstillinge, Denmark, in 1769: before enclosure. (*Source*: H. Thorpe, 'The influence of enclosure in the form and pattern of rural settlement in Denmark', *Transactions of the Institute of British Geographers*, 17, 1951, p. 118.)

by rapid population growth; certainly there are nineteenth-century examples in Eastern Europe of farms of consolidated, compact blocks of land becoming fragmented in a few generations. Alternatively, when the arable lands of a village were first reclaimed from the medieval forest all the villagers may have contributed to the slow clearance of patches of land; each new block would therefore be divided amongst those who had cleared the land. Others have argued that fragmentation or scattering has advantages; it is, after all, still common throughout much of Asia. If a village's arable consisted of pieces of land of very differing value, village egalitarianism might have required each farmer to have land of each type. Scattering, or fragmentation, might also help avoid the risk of crop failure due to localized climatic hazards such as frost or flood. But few climatic hazards are so localized, and this is more likely to have been an advantage perceived after fragmentation had occurred than a fundamental cause. In some villages the strips were not permanently allocated to one farm or farmer, but redistributed amongst the villagers at intervals. This practice survived into the nineteenth century in parts of Galicia, Hungary and Russia.

The village arable lands were surrounded by woodlands and pasture which were not the property of any one individual but could be used in common by all those who owned arable in the open fields, and sometimes also by those who had only a cottage and a garden. The common lands were used mainly for grazing livestock and received no attention from farmers, although of course, the land did benefit from the dung of the animals grazed there. If livestock numbers increased there were problems of overgrazing. To prevent this, numbers were sometimes limited, or 'stinted'; cottagers and farmers were allowed to graze livestock only in proportion to their acreage of arable. A third element in the land use of the open-field village was meadow, that is, grass by rivers and thus intermittently flooded; the silt improved soil fertility and increased grass growth. This land was shared amongst farmers and cut for hay, which was highly prized, for most medieval and early modern farmers had an acute shortage of livestock feed. In addition to using the meadows and common lands, villagers were allowed to graze the stubble once the harvest had been got in. Most medieval farmers left between a quarter and half of their arable in fallow each year, and the limited vegetation that grew on this would also be grazed. In both cases dung was added to the soil.

The common grazing of stubble and fallow, and the intermixture of parcels of land, required that all villagers followed a common routine, and a village council decided what crops were to be grown, and when.

Disadvantages

In the eighteenth and nineteenth centuries the open fields were thought to be a serious impediment to agricultural improvement. As long as pasture was grazed in common, no one was prepared to improve the grassland, and the absence of hedges or fences prevented selective breeding. The common grazing of fallow land made it difficult for enterprising individuals to introduce new crops that could be grown during the fallow year, such as turnips or clover, although there were certainly cases where such innovation did occur. The intermixture of strips made access difficult – squabbling over rights of way was frequent – and the paths and baulks that separated each parcel occupied a significant part of the total arable. Open fields survived in north-east Poland until after the Second World War, and the paths and boundaries there occupied 5 per cent of the arable area. Intermixture also made it difficult to stop the spread of weeds and disease from one farm to another, and prevented drainage other than by the rudimentary ridge and furrow. The scattering of an individual's strips throughout the fields wasted time in travelling from parcel to parcel, whilst the size and shape of the parcels was a major obstacle to the adoption of machinery.

The progress of enclosure

The farmer in the village community was hampered by collective rules, and the enclosure of the open fields allowed farmers to experiment and improve. Enclosure involved a number of separate changes. The abolition of collective regulations, particularly the right to graze the fallow, began at a comparatively early date and was complete in Western Europe by the end of the nineteenth century. The abolition of common grazing of pasture and the division of this land amongst individuals normally occurred later than the enclosure of open-field arable, and indeed is not complete today in many countries. Finally, the enclosure of the open fields involved the consolidation of fragmented parcels into compact blocks and their enclosure with hedges, fences or walls.

Dating the progress of enclosure in Western Europe is difficult. However, two of its components can be traced, the abolition of fallow and the consolidation of fragmented holdings. Once the right to graze stubble and fallow was abolished, individual farmers could grow crops on the land once required to be left unsown; farmers did not have to utilize fallow, but its decline generally followed enclosure. In England after 1600 the open-field system was found mainly in a belt between the north-east coast and the Isle of Wight and was less common in the south-east and the west. Open fields were enclosed in the seventeenth century by private agreement amongst landowners in a parish, and in the eighteenth and nineteenth centuries by Parliamentary Acts, so that by 1850 few parishes still had open fields. But in 1800, when they were still common, one-fifth of the arable of England was still in fallow; by 1850 the figure was one-tenth, and in 1870 only 4 per cent. In France one-third was still in fallow in the late eighteenth century, one-quarter in 1840 and one-tenth in the 1890s; the abolition of fallow was delayed by the wish of villagers to graze the stubble, which was finally declared illegal by an Act passed only in 1889. Elsewhere in Europe significant amounts of fallow survived into the nineteenth century; thus 15 per cent of Germany's arable was still in fallow in 1878 (see figure 2.4).

The second component of enclosure, the consolidation of fragmented holdings, did not occur everywhere. In Britain enclosure was invariably accompanied by the grouping of an individual's strips into a compact block, and was largely but not entirely achieved by the early nineteenth century. Yet as late as 1941 one-quarter of English farms consisted of two or more separate holdings. Parliamentary Acts also led to the consolidation of holdings in Denmark, mainly in the period 1781–1830; the strips of the village of Østerstillinge had been formed into compact farms between 1788 and 1805 (figure 7.2). In Sweden enclosure was accompanied by consolidation in the first half of the nineteenth century and in Norway in the second half.

Consolidation was also carried out in northern Germany, notably in Hanover. In the rest of Western Europe it made little progress in the nineteenth century. In France in 1882 the average farm still consisted of 22 dispersed parcels, and fragmentation also remained extreme in Belgium and much of south-west and southern Germany. In a village near Würzburg, in Lower Franconia, for example, farms before consolidation in the 1950s averaged only 1.4 hectares and consisted of 25.8 parcels, each of 0.06 hectares. So slow had been the progress of consolidation that in the 1950s it was estimated that between one-third and one-half of Europe's arable land was still unconsolidated. The amount of land still requiring consolidation varied greatly: in Sweden and Denmark it was only 5 per cent, but 50 per cent in West Germany and Spain. It was the

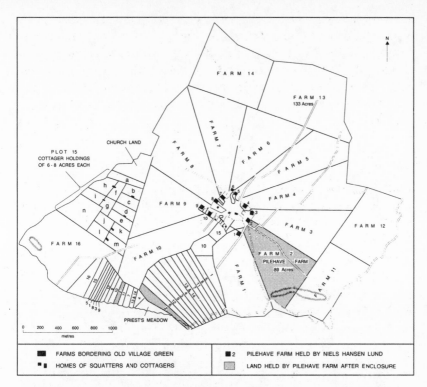

Figure 7.2 The township of Østerstillinge, Denmark, in 1805: after enclosure. (*Source*: H. Thorpe, 'The influence of enclosure in the form and pattern of rural settlement in Denmark', *Transactions of the Institute of British Geographers*, 17, 1951, p. 119.)

need to use machinery that accelerated consolidation schemes in the post-war period.

In Britain, Denmark and Sweden, the change in the composition of holdings led to a change in the settlement pattern. In the open-field community, farm buildings were sited in the village (figure 7.1) and farmers went out to their scattered holdings from this central point. After consolidation, the new compact farms were often at some distance from the village. Thus farmers moved slowly out from the village to live on their new farms, and the former nuclear pattern of rural settlement gave way to a depopulated village and scattered farms (figure 7.3).

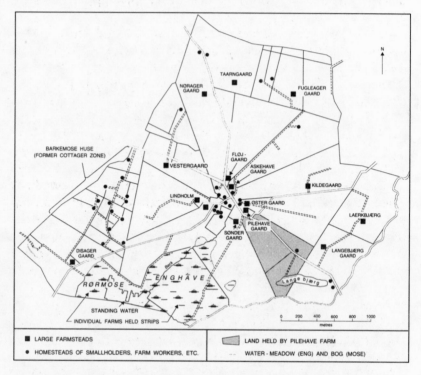

Figure 7.3 The township of Østerstillinge, Denmark, 1893: after relocation of some farmhouses. (*Source*: H. Thorpe, 'The influence of enclosure in the form and pattern of rural settlement in Denmark', *Transactions of the Institute of British Geographers*, 17, p. 126.)

Europe overseas

Settlement by Europeans overseas began well before the completion of peasant emancipation in Europe. However, the systems of land ownership overseas bore few marks of medieval systems of land ownership, at least in North America and Australasia. The earliest settlements in North America were in Quebec, where some elements of the French seignorial system were transferred, in New England, where aspects of English village communities were maintained, and in Virginia, where later slavery changed the pattern of life throughout the whole South. But most of the rest of North America was settled without the medieval impediments to progress that characterized so much of Europe. Farms were rarely fragmented and the abundance of land meant that they were much larger than in Europe.

Although landlords and tenants were to be found, there was no question of the feudal relationship which persisted in Europe until well into the nineteenth century, although of course slavery remained in the South until its abolition in 1863, which occurred at about the same time as serfdom ended in Russia. Until the 1820s farm settlement in the United States was largely to the east of the Appalachians. Thereafter the expansion of settlement was rapid and the federal government had to devise means of disposing of a vast public domain. Much squatting was retrospectively legalized by the Preemption Acts. In 1862 the Homestead Act allowed any American to claim 160 acres (65 ha), conditional only upon improvement. But the Homestead Act disposed of only a small part of the land that was alienated in the nineteenth century. Land grants were made to railroads between 1850 and 1870, much of which was sold to farmers, and each state received land which it rented or sold to raise funds, particularly for schools and colleges. A great deal more of American land became tenant-farmed than had been intended; in 1910 only half the farmers were full owners of their land, even though the cost of acquisition by farmers had been remarkably low. In 1872 the Canadian government passed a Land Act similar to the Homestead Act; after 1890 much of the prairie passed into the hands of occupier-owners, again at low cost, so that three-quarters of all Canadian farmers were occupier-owners by 1941. Since then there has been some decline, but only because occupier-owners seeking to increase the size of their farms have had to rent extra land.

In Australia the Crown laid claim to the whole continent, and only a small percentage of this has passed into private ownership. The great grazing areas are held on long leases from the Crown, although much of this leasehold can be sold and inherited. The settlement by farmers rather than graziers was encouraged by state laws, beginning in New South Wales in 1861, that allowed claims for Crown land at £1 an acre. As a consequence most of the agricultural holdings are owner-occupied – nine-tenths in 1970.

Thus neither North American or Australia had the problems of serfdom or of collective village farming to overcome, while the dispersal of land at reasonable prices meant that capital could be invested in improvements rather than in acquiring land.

Conclusions

The slow freeing of the peasant from both the feudal landlord and
the village collective was a necessary prerequisite for modernization. However, the retarding effect of these institutions in Western
Europe may have been exaggerated. Most of the disadvantages of
feudal tenure had lapsed before its formal abolition in the eighteenth and nineteenth centuries. Nor did the drawbacks of the open
fields prevent the adoption of the agricultural innovation of the
early modern period; the acute fragmentation of farms, however,
did become an obstacle once machinery became necessary.

8
Scale, Structure and Organization

The post-war period has seen two striking changes in the organization of farming in the West. First, the size of farms has become greater; by this is meant not the unit of ownership, for a landlord's estate may be divided into many farms, each worked independently of the landlord, but the unit of production. The decision-maker is the farmer, and not the landlord. Second, an increasing proportion of the farmer's inputs has come to be purchased from manufacturing industry, and much of the food produced on farms is now processed in factories before reaching the customer.

The measurement of farm size

In the nineteenth century many observers believed that farms were getting larger. Indeed some, notably Karl Marx, believed that the small farm was an obstacle to progress in agriculture and that the creation of large farms worked by hired labourers rather than the family was a prerequisite for agricultural growth. Unfortunately, there was at the time little statistical information on the size of farms in Europe or North America to confirm the rise of the large farm; it was not until the 1880s that agricultural censuses collected information. But even when national censuses began to provide statistics on farm size, interpretation was fraught with difficulties. In some cases ownership and farm size were confused. Also, differences exist between censuses in the type of land counted when determining farm size; in some countries woodland was included, in others rough grazing, whilst in many countries only improved land was counted. But perhaps the most important variation was in the minimum size of agricultural holding to be included in the census. Some censuses included all holdings of agricultural land, others excluded those below a certain size.

Most farm-size data is available in the form of tables which show

Table 8.1   Farm structure in Western Europe *c*.1930

	0–10 ha		10–50 ha		over 50 ha	
	Numbers[a]	Area[b]	Numbers	Area	Numbers	Area
Switzerland	80.0	50.0	19.5	43.0	0.5	7.0
Belgium	81.0	45.0	18.0	46.0	1.0	9.0
Netherlands	66.5	31.5	32.0	60.0	1.5	8.5
France	62.0	20.0	34.0	50.0	4.0	30.0
Germany	62.0	22.0	33.0	46.0	5.0	32.0
Denmark	52.0	16.5	46.0	68.0	2.0	15.5
England and Wales	35.0	6.7	41.7	28.1	23.3	65.2

[a] Number of holdings in size class as percentage of all holdings.
[b] Area of agricultural land in size class as percentage of all agricultural land.
Source: P. Lamartine Yates, *Food Production in Western Europe*, London, 1940, pp. 52, 129, 203, 274, 361, 438.

the number of farms in specific size classes; to make comparisons possible, such data are usually presented as percentages of the total number of holdings (table 8.1). But whilst in most European countries a large proportion of farms falls into the smaller categories, the *area* occupied by such farms may be a much smaller proportion of the total area. Thus, though the small farm may be the most common, most of the area may be cultivated by medium or large farms. Thus in France in 1930 only 4 per cent of all holdings exceeded 50 hectares, but these occupied 30 per cent of the agricultural area (table 8.1).

The significance of farm size

The size of farms is important for a number of reasons. First, the amount of land available to a farmer is a prime – although not the only – determinant of his possible total output. In a subsistence society an inadequate amount of food may be produced; in commercial farming, size, among other things, determines the net income of the family. That a high proportion of all West European farms have been very small is a major cause of rural poverty; many small farms have been unable to provide an adequate income, and their occupiers have had to seek extra income from other jobs, such as working as labourers on neighbouring and larger farms, by undertaking handicrafts – particularly in textiles – or in the nineteenth and twentieth centuries by working in factories.

There have been various estimates of the minimum size of holding necessary to provide a subsistence income; 5 or 10 hectares are the most commonly cited, and it is clear that prior to the nineteenth century many farms were far smaller than this. With the rise of manufacturing industry in the nineteenth century an additional problem arose. In nearly all of Europe and North America there was – and continues to be – a marked difference between the average income earned in agriculture and that earned in manufacturing, mining and service activities. Indeed the greater incomes to be earned in these activities attracted first labourers and more recently farmers to the towns. Between the 1850s and the 1950s average farm incomes were often no more than half those in non-agricultural activities. Thus attention has been paid to the minimum size of farm that can provide the farmer with an income comparable with that of an industrial worker. In West Germany in the 1960s this was estimated to be 20 hectares; but at that time only 10 per cent of all holdings exceeded 20 hectares, for Western Europe has inherited from the past a large number of very small farms. The extent of the problem is indicated in table 8.2, which shows that a high proportion of holdings were under 20 hectares in 1975, and that much of the farm population was concentrated on these small farms. In this Western Europe is different from the more recently settled lands of North America and Australia.

A second reason for the importance of farm size is that it influences productivity. Productivity is a function of such factors as management skills or the capital available, but certain advantages accrue to large farms as against small, which are described by economists as economies of scale. For example, both small and large farms need buildings to shelter livestock and store food, but the cost of these per hectare is higher on a small farm than on a large one. Again, even today many European farms are too small to employ family labour fully throughout the year, and so output per man is much lower than on larger farms; on the other hand, because of the abundance of labour available, farming on small farms is intensive, and both inputs and output per hectare are

Table 8.2   Western Europe: small farms and their importance, 1975

	(A)	(B)	(C)
Italy	94.2	52.0	90.8
Belgium	78.8	45.0	74.4
Netherlands	76.8	45.9	73.4
Germany	76.5	40.8	72.8
Ireland	62.8	27.7	55.9
Denmark	59.6	25.8	53.6
France	58.6	20.3	51.4
Luxembourg	50.4	17.7	43.0
United Kingdom	40.4	6.1	29.8

A: Percentage of all farms which are 1 ha but less than 20 ha.
B: Percentage of total agricultural area occupied by them.
C: Percentage of total active farm population engaged thereon, 1975.
Source: J. Scully, 'The evolution of farm structures in the Community', in M. Tracy and I. Hodac (eds), *Prospects for Agriculture in the European Economic Community*, Bruges, 1979, pp. 139–61.

normally higher than on large farms (figure 8.1). Yet again, modern farm machinery, with the exception of the tractor, is adapted to specific crops, and is therefore only used for a short period of the year, and so machines are generally only economic if a large acreage is devoted to the particular crop. For example, the first combine harvesters in England were uneconomic on farms which had less than 120 hectares in grain. Since then the threshold has fallen; by the 1960s combines paid if only 40 hectares was in grain. Before the age of machines, similar principles applied to the use of horses and ploughs, which could not be maintained in order to plough very small holdings, so the spade was used instead.

Finally, large farms are often said to have advantages in borrowing, in purchasing inputs, and in marketing. Thus the occupiers of large farms might find it easier to borrow from banks to finance improvements, and are able to gain discounts from the suppliers of fertilizers and to make advantageous arrangements with the purchasers of their products because they have large quantities to sell. In Europe these disadvantages were partly overcome in the late nineteenth century by the rise of the co-operative movement. In

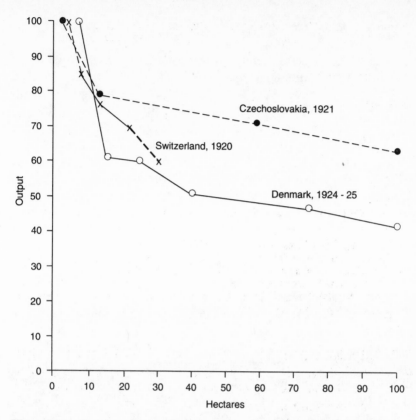

Figure 8.1 Gross output per hectare by farm size class: Czechoslovakia, Switzerland and Denmark in the 1920s (output of the smallest size class is represented by 100). (*Source*: P. A. Sorokin, C. C. Zimmerman and C. J. Galpin (eds), *A Systematic Sourcebook of Rural Sociology*, vol. I, 1965, pp. 390–1.)

Germany the pioneer was F. W. Raiffeisen who founded co-operative banks for farmers in the 1850s; they later became purchasing and marketing co-operatives, and by 1914 had 6 million members. Co-operatives for marketing produce were an important innovation in the late nineteenth century, particularly in the Netherlands and Denmark, whilst purchasing co-operatives became widespread in the early part the twentieth century. Agricultural co-operatives did not develop in the home of the co-operative movement, England, possibly because of the larger size of farms.

Trends in farm size

Before the nineteenth century there are no national statistics on farm size; such limited evidence as there is refers only to small areas and often only exists for one year, so there are great difficulties in establishing what happened over time. The beginnings of modern variations in farm size go back to the Middle Ages, when villeins received land in return for the services due to the seignior. This was a taxation unit as well as a means of subsistence for the villein and his family, and varied in size throughout Europe; in France and England it usually fell between 6 and 12 hectares. Families had in addition access to the common grazing and woodland. The demesne of the seignior was much larger, and as early as the twelfth and thirteenth centuries there were also many cottagers with only a hectare or so of land, so that there was a considerable range in farm size. Two forces led to later change; population growth reduced farm size, particularly in areas where partible inheritance was practised, and the farm divided amongst all children at the death of the farmer; second, particularly after the establishment of a market in peasant land, was the tendency for the more efficient or more fortunate to acquire extra land. It has been argued that farms got smaller in the thirteenth century, when population growth was pressing upon resources in much of Western Europe, and again in the sixteenth century.

What scattered evidence there is on farm size before the nineteenth century suggests that farms were predominantly small (table 8.3); indeed, a very large proportion were less than 5 hectares, and so not large enough to provide an adequate living. Conversely, farms over 20 hectares were a small fraction of all holdings, although they occupied a greater proportion of the area.

By the late eighteenth century there are signs of regional divergences in the size of farms. Farms had been getting larger in England since the seventeenth century. Landlords slowly added small and uneconomic holdings together and enclosure, which was expensive, led to the decline of small landowners and the absorption of their farms into larger units. In nineteenth-century Denmark and Sweden enclosure was also accompanied by an increase in farm size. In east Germany serfs had to surrender part of their land to their lords in return for freedom, and so the demesne, after

Table 8.3 Examples of pre-nineteenth-century farm size structure (percentage of all farms)

Savoy, 16th c. (hectares)	%		Sainte-Croix, France, 16th c. (hectares)	%
Under 1	52.4		Under 5	38.8
1–5	34.7		5–10	28.8
5–10	7.3		10–25	25.0
10–25	3.9		Over 25	7.4
Over 25	1.7			100.0
	100.0			

Saxony (hectares)	%		Hochberg, Germany, 1788 (hectares)	%
Under 5	32.1		Under 0.7	45.0
5–20	51.8		0.7–2.9	39.0
20–100	14.3		2.9–5.8	11.0
Over 100	1.8		Over 5.8	5.4
	100.0			100.0

Bohemia, early 18th c. (hectares)	%		E. England, c.1280 (hectares)	%
Under 1.5	35.7		Under 3	32.7
1.5–4.5	21.0		3	9.6
4.5–8.5	17.4			31.2
8.5–17.5	20.4		12	24.0
Over 17.5	5.5		Over 12	2.5
	100.0			100.0

Sources: J. Blum, *The End of the Old Order in Europe*, Princeton, 1978, pp. 106–9; B. H. Slicher van Bath, *The Agrarian History of Western Europe AD 500–1850*, London, 1963, pp. 134–6; N. J. G. Pounds, *An Historical Geography of Europe 1500–1840*, Cambridge, 1979, pp. 168–70; A. Klima, 'Agrarian class structure and economic development in pre-industrial Bohemia', in T. H. Aston and C. H. E. Philpin (eds), *The Brenner Debate: Agrarian Class Structure and Economic Development in Pre-Industrial Europe*, Cambridge, 1985.

the emancipation of 1807, became an even larger farm, worked by landless labourers. But in much of the rest of Europe there was no increase in farm size, and in Germany, Belgium and the Netherlands the average size of farm declined in the nineteenth century. In the late nineteenth century, the small farm was still predominant except in England (table 8.4). The early part of the twentieth century did not see radical changes, although the number of very small holdings was declining in England and France. But of course trends in the *number* of farms does not indicate the proportion of farmland occupied by farms of different size. By the 1930s the small farm (less than 10 hectares) occupied half the farmland in Belgium and Switzerland (table 8.1), whilst the medium-sized farm (10–50 hectares) was predominant in the Netherlands and France; the large farm (over 50 hectares) was dominant only in England, although also important in northern France and east Germany. The modern distribution of farm size (figure 8.2) was probably apparent by the early nineteenth century.

Farm size overseas

Farm size in the European-settled areas overseas was very different. Eastern North America had been settled from the seventeenth century, but population densities were much lower than in Western Europe and agricultural holdings larger, although the absence of machinery precluded the existence of very large holdings. In the United States after 1820, in Australia from the 1860s and in Canada from the 1880s, agricultural settlement advanced into sparsely settled areas; by this time machinery was available and indeed necessary. Land settlement policies made the acquisition of comparatively large areas possible, and the farms established in these regions were larger than those in the older settled areas, and far larger than those in Western Europe; only in England did average farm size approach that in the overseas countries. Yet in spite of the advance into sparsely populated areas, farm size structure did not greatly change in these countries during the nineteenth century. But from the 1920s and 1930s there were the beginnings of radical change; these were bad years for food-exporting nations, with over-production and falling prices, and many small farmers went bankrupt. More significantly, the availability of new machines

Table 8.4   Data on farm size from early agricultural censuses (number of holdings)

Germany, 1882 (hectares)	%	Ireland 1845 (hectares)	%	France 1892 (hectares)	%
Under 2	58.0	0.4–2.0	23.6	Under 1	39.2
2–5	18.6	2–6	40.5	1–5	32.1
5–20	17.6	Over 6	35.9	5–10	13.8
20–50	4.5		100.0	10–40	12.5
Over 50	1.3			Over 40	2.4
	100.0				100.0

Sweden, 1890 (hectares)	%	Norway 1850 (hectares)	%
Under 2	22.5	Under 5	80.0
2–20	66.3		
20–100	10.2		
Over 100	1.0		
	100.0		

USA, 1880 (hectares)	%	England and Wales 1851 (hectares)	%
1.2–3.6	3.3	2.0–8.1	19.7
4.0–19.8	25.9	8.1–20.0	21.8
20.0–40.0	25.8	20.0–40.5	20.7
40.5–202	42.3	40.5–121.5	30.0
Over 202	2.7	Over 121.5	7.8
	100.0		100.0

Sources: H. J. Puhle 'Lords and peasants in the Kaiserreich', in R. G. Moeller (ed.), *Peasants and Lords in Modern Germany: Recent Studies in Agricultural History*, London, 1986, p. 84; D. Grigg, *Population Growth and Agrarian Change: An Historical Perspective*, Cambridge, 1980, pp. 171, 195, 212.

and the rapid adoption of the tractor increased the optimum economic size of farms. The gap between farm and non-farm incomes persisted and the low incomes of farmers started a great exodus, particularly amongst those with a small farm business. Thus in the United States in 1920 there were 3,780,000 farms of less than 40 hectares; by 1969 there were only 1,095,000. The larger farms –

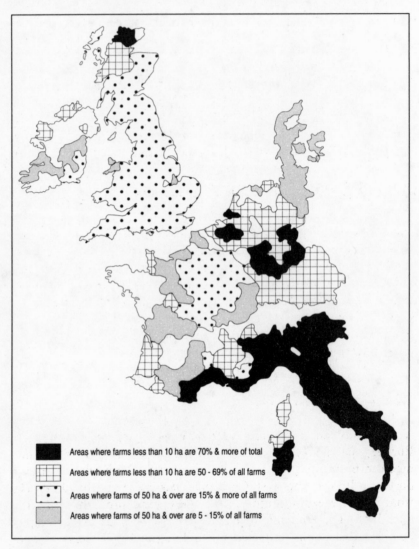

Figure 8.2 The distribution of small and large farms in Western Europe.
(*Source*: R. Calmes, 'L'évolution des structures d'exploitation dans les pays de la
C.E.E.', *Annals de Géographie*, 90, 1981, pp. 401–27.)

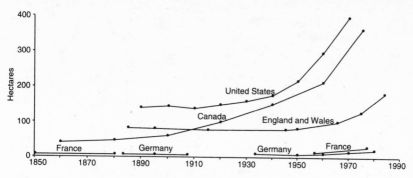

Figure 8.3 Average size of farm in selected countries.

over 200 hectares – occupied one-twelfth of the agricultural land in the country in 1920, two-thirds in 1969. The average size of farm in the United States more than doubled between 1940 and 1970, as did that of Canada (figure 8.3). This inevitably led to a concentration of agricultural output into fewer hands. By 1981 6 per cent of Canadian farms accounted for 38 per cent of the gross output, whilst 1 per cent of farms in the United States produced two-thirds of net farm income.

Western Europe since 1945

In 1945 mechanization had made only slow progress in Western Europe; the size of farms had probably changed little since the nineteenth century, and outside England, Denmark, Sweden, northern France and east Germany, was not radically different from the eighteenth century. But there were profound changes after 1945. The economic revival of industry and the higher wages obtained in factories attracted not only agricultural workers, but many small farmers; increasingly sons and daughters refused to carry on working on small farms when their parents retired or died, and those who did stay combined farming with some other job.

The fall in the labour force led to the rapid mechanization of West European farming, and this in turn required larger farms for optimum efficiency. West European farming has failed to adapt to the economic needs of mechanization; a majority of the farms are still too small to utilize machines fully or to provide an adequate

Table 8.5   Farm size structure in Europe, North America and Australasia in 1970 (percentage of total number of holdings and of total agricultural area)

	Under 5 ha		5–20 ha		20–100 ha		Over 100 ha	
	Number	Area	Number	Area	Number	Area	Number	Area
Australasia	13.1	0.0	13.9	0.1	25.6	1.0	47.4	98.9
North America	7.0	0.1	14.9	1.2	45.4	14.8	32.7	83.9
Europe	66.0	13.7	26.5	32.6	6.9	28.6	0.6	25.1

Sources: World Bank, *World Development Report 1982*, Washington DC, 1982.

income. But there have been dramatic changes. The number of small holdings has fallen and the average size has increased. Between 1950 and 1979 the number of farms in West Germany declined by 850,000, and in the Netherlands the number of farms halved between 1950 and 1980. The average size everywhere has increased. But this has not removed the difference between the farm size structure of Western Europe and that of European-settled countries overseas (table 8.5).

By 1970 nearly all the agricultural area of North America and Australia was in farms of more than 100 hectares, but only one quarter of Europe, whilst two-thirds of Europe's farms comprised less than 5 hectares, but only 13 per cent of Australia's and 7 per cent of North America's. But the decline of the small farm has certainly not come to an end, even in the United States. By the 1970s it was estimated that a minimum of 400 hectares was necessary to gain all the possible economies of scale in farming in the Corn Belt. To achieve this, 60 per cent of the existing farms would have to disappear.

The organization of food production

In traditional agriculture farmers consumed much of their own output and most of their inputs were produced on the farm. But with the increase in the proportion of the population living in towns there was need for a much more elaborate system of food marketing. From the seventeenth century internal transport systems increased and improved, connecting the farms with distant urban markets; farmers slowly ceased to carry their produce to market, and carriers took over this task. In the cities there was a need for retailers – food shops – and between the retailers and the producers wholesalers emerged to deal with the more complex flows of foodstuffs. There was also a tendency for activities once undertaken in the home to be done by intermediaries. This is most notably illustrated by the slow decline of home brewing of beer and home baking. In the early nineteenth century most rural households bought flour from the small corn mills, and baked bread, cakes and biscuits at home. Home baking was replaced by commercial bakeries, but it has taken a long time. Indeed, in the United States home baking accounted for more than half of total output until the 1930s.

Since the late 1880s convenience foods have become increasingly important. The food industries have combined raw materials that were once mixed at home to produce sauces, pickles, jams, cakes, and since the 1950s pre-cooked dishes. Thus since the eighteenth century a growing proportion of farm output has had to move through the wholesale and retail networks, while much of what was once domestic food preparation has moved from the kitchen to the factory.

There have been equally dramatic changes at the other end of the food production chain. Traditional farmers used inputs produced on their own farms. Thus the seed sown came from the previous harvest, fertilizers from the dung of animals kept on the farm, and power was limited to the muscle of animals, men and women. Even farm implements were made on the farm, although some particular villagers might specialize in this. Animals were fed on the commons and the fallow, and from the seventeenth century on crops such as turnips grown on the farm.

In the subsistence, self-sufficient economy there was little movement of goods and money across the boundaries of the farm, and certainly little across the boundaries of the village community, although there had always been some connection with the outside world; some produce had to be sold to pay taxes and buy the salt, metals and other necessities that might not be locally produced. But with the modernization of agriculture many of the activities once carried out on the farm or by the village community came to be undertaken by people other than farmers. In effect there was an increasing division of labour, and farmers became specialized in farming. The transport and sale of their produce went to intermediaries, and local people began to specialize as craftsmen, more capable than farmers of making implements or wagons or repairing buildings.

The rise of the input industries

Comparatively little is known of the early history of the input industries, other than the manufacture of agricultural machinery and chemical fertilizers. But slowly farmers began to purchase an increasing proportion of their inputs from off the farm. Thus in Sweden in the 1860s purchases by farmers from outside the farm sector accounted for only 5 per cent of the gross value of farm incomes, but by 1950 this proportion had reached 30 per cent (figure 1.3), and in the 1970s it exceeded 50 per cent in most developed countries. There are still very marked regional variations in the amount of inputs purchased from off the farm in 1960; the higher the proportion of inputs purchased, the greater the inputs per man and per hectare, and usually the higher the output *per capita* (table 8.6).

The rise of the input industries was closely connected with the industrial revolution. The early chemical industries concentrated on the production of dyes for the textile industry and added the production of chemical fertilizers in the 1850s after the first production of superphosphate, which required sulphuric acid, a basic product of the early chemical industries. The discovery of a means of fixing atmospheric nitrogen into a nitrate usable as a fertilizer in 1909 was a fundamental advance; the chemical industries in the inter-war period, but particularly after 1945, also began to produce insecticides, fungicides and pesticides.

In most of Western Europe agricultural implements were handmade from wood by local craftsmen until the eighteenth century. The advances in the technology of iron production in Britain in the eighteenth century and the reduction of the real cost of iron led to the greater use of iron in making implements; the first all-iron plough was made at Rotherham in the 1770s. The emergence of factories making standard implements mainly from iron dates from the period after the end of the Napoleonic Wars. British expertise

Table 8.6 Inputs and output per worker, c.1960

	Inputs bought from outside agriculture as % of value of output	Fertilizers, kg per hectare of arable land	Tractor h.p. per 100 workers	Output in wheat units per agricultural worker
Britain	53	180	1274	355
The Netherlands	43	556	415	314
USA	42	38	3060	706
France	21	102	413	183
Poland	14	49	23	82
Spain	11	32	27	63
India	2	2	0.5	11

Source: W. Rozlucki, 'The Green Revolution and the development of traditional agriculture: a case study of India', *Geographia Polonica*, 35, 1977, p. 112.

in steam engine manufacture and the invention of the threshing machine in 1786 ensured that the British agricultural engineering industry dominated machine-making until the 1850s and 1860s, when farm machinery made in the United States and Germany began to challenge. The invention of the tractor and the combine harvester has given the United States a leading role for much of the twentieth century.

Machinery does not, surprisingly, account for a large proportion of the modern farmer's expenditure. In Britain by far the largest item is the purchase of feeding stuffs. In the eighteenth and early nineteenth centuries roots and grass grown on the farm provided most animal feed, but from the 1820s Britain began to import oilseeds; once the oil had been extracted, the residue was used as oil-cake to feed cattle, and later in the century imported grains, particularly maize, were fed to animals. Only small amounts of home grain were fed to livestock, but some such grain was purchased by feed compounders, who provided feeds which varied in composition and origin according to the price of the various grain or oilseeds used. By the 1920s compounders were producing animal rations, designed to provide the requisite nutritional content for different animals at different ages, and since 1945 an increasing proportion of home-grown grain has been fed to animals. In most countries in Western Europe and North America at least half of cereal output is sold to compounders. The provision of feeds has allowed many livestock producers with only small farms to survive and has been the basis of the rise of highly specialized broiler and pig production.

Little is known about the origins of seed merchants, nor is it known how farmers changed from producing their own seed to purchasing it. But the remarkable advances in plant breeding in this century ensured that farmers purchased seed so as to benefit from higher yields and greater immunity to disease. By the 1970s British farmers' expenditure on seed was as great as on fuel – 6.5 per cent – but was dwarfed by the expenditure upon feedstuffs, 58 per cent of the total. Indeed, although the purchase of power off the farm in the form of tractors, self-propelled machines, oil and electricity, and the remarkable increases in power *per capita*, have transformed farming, these items make up only a surprisingly small item – about a fifth – of modern farm expenditure in Britain.

The processing of agricultural production

Much emphasis has been put by modern writers upon the rise of
modern factory food processing, and its great importance in the
food production system. Indeed, by 1980 – if slaughtering is included – 85 per cent of the output of British farms was processed.
But processing is not new; much of the food raised upon traditional
farms had to be processed in some way before it reached the
consumer. This is most obvious with cotton, wool, flax and hides,
all of which are sold to textile manufactures or tanneries. But it was
also true of food products, some of which had to be processed
before they could be used. The grinding of corn in mills, rather
than in querns, has been common practice for the last millennium,
but most of the mills were small and driven by wind or water;
while feudalism prevailed serfs often had to have their grain ground
in the seignior's mill. Malt had to be extracted from barley, and
until the nineteenth century breweries were widely distributed
throughout Western Europe; wine was commonly made on the
farms that grew the grapes. Butter and cheese were, until the
mid-nineteenth century, produced entirely upon farms. At first
potatoes, which were not widely grown in Western Europe until
the eighteenth century, were eaten by people and pigs; but very
soon alcohol and starch were extracted from the crop.
  In the early nineteenth century most processing was small-scale
and took place either on the farm or in mills or presses that served
only local communities. But from then onwards there were major
changes in the location and scale of food processing, so that by the
1950s most processing took place away from the farm, and the
farmer was essentially producing raw materials for factories.
  The first break with farming came with the early sugar beet
factories in Silesia and northern France; the British blockade of
Europe during the Napoleonic Wars cut the continent off from the
supply of cane sugar, so sugar beet production was subsidized by
Napoleon. Individual farms could not produce enough beet to
make it economic to have their own sugar refinery, and factories
were built in Saxony, Silesia, northern France and the Netherlands. There was a further stimulus to processing at this time. In
1810 Nicolas Appert showed that heating and sealing food could

preserve its quality. Appert sealed his foods in bottles with a cork, but the principle was almost at once applied in Britain with the tin can as container. Initially much of the tinned food was supplied to soldiers and expeditions. It was not until the mid-nineteenth century that the meat-packing industry in the United States emerged and was soon emulated in Australasia and Argentina. It was also in the United States that the canning of fruit and vegetables developed in the 1870s and 1880s. Florida and California had ideal climatic conditions for production, but the major markets were in the cities of the north-east; the canneries resolved this problem. In Britain a different solution was adopted. Combining sugar and fruit and sealing in jars retarded the decay of fruit, and as jams were cheaper than butter they had a wide sale in the late nineteenth century. In the 1870s and 1880s the decline of grain prices encouraged some farmers to turn to fruit production, and jam (and marmalade) production grew rapidly.

A more profound change was taking place on dairy farms at this time. Until the 1840s milk was sold fresh where markets were nearby, but most milk production was converted to cheese or butter on the farm. In that decade a number of cheese factories were opened in Ohio. By the 1860s and 1870s American cheese was being exported, and prompted the opening of factories in Western Europe. Butter production was also rapidly transferred to factories; indeed, because steam power could be applied to churning, the transfer from farm to factory was more rapid than that of cheese-making. Even so, in the United States one-quarter of all butter was still made on the farm in 1930. Other ways were found to prolong the life of milk; from the 1850s condensed tinned milk was produced, and later evaporated milk. The distribution of fresh milk was also profoundly changed as refrigeration, the railway and the milk churn allowed milk to be sent much greater distances to market. In Britain an elaborate system of wholesaling and retailing allowed the delivery of fresh milk to the doorstep each day.

The milling of flour and the production of beer exemplify other trends in food processing. Neither had been customarily produced on farms, but both were locally produced; in the eighteenth century most English mills drew their grain from no more than ten miles (16 km) away. The application of steam power to milling – there were fifty-five steam-driven corn mills by 1805 – and the adoption of new milling methods, notably in the 1870s, gave the larger factory great advantages, and local mills in Britain and North America gave way to large merchant millers. In Britain many of these were located in ports, because much British flour was milled from imported high-protein grains.

In the United States in the 1920s Clarence Birdseye developed the method of quick freezing: used at first for fish, it was rapidly extended to fruit and vegetables. Rather earlier, the convenience food processors – factories that combined or modified the raw materials provided by farmers, and saved the housewife much time – emerged; breakfast cereals are but one of these products, and more recently pre-cooked foods have become important.

Agriculture and the food production system

The decline of agricultural employment is one of the distinctive features of economic development. Over the last two hundred years the proportion of the population engaged in food production on the farm has fallen from three-quarters to less than one-twentieth. Yet over the same period activities once undertaken on farms have been transferred to the industrial sector. In many countries the numbers engaged in processing and distributing food now exceeds those directly employed in food production on the farm. In Britain in 1981, 2.1 per cent of the labour force worked on farms, 2.3 per cent in food processing and 3.75 per cent in food distribution. The numbers employed in providing inputs is more difficult to calculate, but in 1955, before the major expansion in the use of machinery, fertilizers and power, the numbers so employed nearly equalled those in direct production in the United Kingdom (table 8.7).

In the nineteenth century it was common for firms manufacturing finished products to extend financial control over the supply of raw materials, most notably in the case of the steel industry, where steel firms bought blast furnaces and iron ore mines. This was hardly known in agriculture in Western Europe, but was common in plantation agriculture, particularly where the crop was processed. In the production of many crops such as sugar cane or rubber, one company controlled the agricultural production and

Table 8.7   Labour force engaged in agricultural production per 1000 ha of agricultural land, 1955

	(A) Numbers directly in agriculture	(B) Numbers indirectly in agriculture	B as percentage of A
United Kingdom	78	72	0.92
West Germany	134	73	0.54
Denmark	115	53	0.46
Belgium	165	75	0.45
Sweden	108	32	0.3
France	93	24	0.29
Italy	317	60	0.19
Greece, Portugal and Spain	241	34	0.14

Source: J. F. Dewhurst, J. O. Coppock and P. L. Yates, *Europe's Needs and Resources*, New York, 1962, p. 195.

the processing, and in some cases owned the ships that took the refined or partially processed products to the markets in North America and Western Europe.

There was little sign before the twentieth century that food manufacturers would extend their control backwards to the raising of crops and livestock. Sugar beet factories in France, Germany, and England in the early twentieth century, which made contracts with farmers to grow specific amounts and to deliver the crop at specific times, were an exception. This form of contracting spread with the use of frozen and canned vegetables in Britain in the 1920s, and since 1945 has become common in the production of vegetables for freezing. Contracting allows the processor to ensure quality and the timing of production. In Britain processors do not commonly buy farms to ensure a supply of raw materials. In the United States much has been made of the rise of agribusiness, where processors do control farm output. It is particularly widespread in the production of poultry, vegetables and beef. However, 85 per cent of American farms are still owned by families and three-quarters of the farms recorded as corporately owned are simply family farms registered as corporations for tax purposes.

Nonetheless, many believe this type of organization will increase in the future.

Conclusions

The modernization of agriculture has had surprisingly little effect on the size of production units, although the decline of the small farm has been universal since 1950. The organization of food production has, however, changed dramatically; great specialization in the many links in the food system has improved overall efficiency. Industrialization has driven these changes, providing inputs, allowing advantage to be taken of economies of scale, and indirectly by raising consumer incomes, which has led to far more processing of food before it reaches the kitchen.

9

Science, the State and the Diffusion of Knowledge

Agricultural productivity can be increased in a variety of ways. For example, nineteenth-century landlords could increase the productivity of the farms they rented by increasing their size, and so allowing economies of scale to be gained, or by replacing an incompetent tenant by an efficient one. But much of the increase in physical productivity has been the result of the adoption of new technical methods. This needs a broad interpretation. A new technique can be an implement – the introduction, for example, of the scythe – or a new crop, such as sugar beet. But it can also be an idea, such as that of growing crops alternately in a rotation.

There are a number of stages in the introduction of a new technique into farming. In the modern world it may begin with a discovery in pure science. Thus the spread of new varieties of cereals was dependent upon the much earlier discovery of the principles of genetics by Gregor Mendel in the 1860s. But there is invariably a lag between the fundamental scientific advance and its application upon farms. Thus, for example, in the case of hybrid corn, a number of further discoveries in genetics were necessary – the crossing techniques for producing hybrid corn plants, further advances in the knowledge of inheritance, and the invention of the double-cross method of mass seed production. These were achieved in the United States between 1900 and 1919. The adoption of the new seeds also required a demand from farmers, which was brought about by the declining yield obtained from existing corn varieties. But the mere existence of a tested and approved technique such as hybrid corn seed did not lead to its immediate and universal adoption.

Most innovations are adopted at first only by the better educated farmers, and those with larger acreages, and for some time only a small proportion of farmers will try the new technique. There then follows a sharp increase in the rate of adoption until only the less well-informed farmers have not adopted it. How new techniques spread depends upon a variety of factors. Farmers hear about innovations in different ways. Some learn of them from books or journals, others from extension officers, others – perhaps a majority – from observing their neighbours' fields. There have been crucial changes in the way in which inventions have been made and transmitted to farmers; some of the more important issues are discussed in this chapter.

Science and agriculture

In the last thirty years many of the technical advances in agriculture have been the result of the applications of discoveries in genetics and biochemistry. It is less easy to trace the relationship between science and agriculture in the past. Scientific advance implies a full and correct understanding of how a particular natural process works. But two qualifications must be made. First, farmers may be aware of a technique and apply it, without fully understanding how it works; there can of course be technical advance without scientific progress. Thus, for example, more than two thousand years ago Greek farmers were aware of the value of growing legumes and their effect upon soil fertility and crop yields; but the significance of bacteria and the nodules on the roots of leguminous plants in fixing nitrogen were not understood until the late nineteenth century. Second, existing knowledge may be incorrect. Thus Jethro Tull believed that plant nutrients were contained in soil particles, that roots absorbed particles, and that the finer the particle the greater the chance the roots of a crop had of absorbing nutrients. He thus argued that soil should be frequently cultivated to produce a fine tilth. It was not until the 1940s that it was realized that the only value of cultivation was to destroy weeds. Justus von Liebig's book *Chemistry and its Application to Agriculture*, published in 1840, was a remarkable stimulus to applied research, yet von Liebig believed that crops received sufficient nitrogen from rain and so only mineral fertilizers were necessary to increase crop yields.

Prior to the nineteenth century the progress of agriculture owed little to advances in science. Most improvement came from the adoption of the better practices of the more enterprising farmers, and they in turn relied upon their own observation and the accumulated wisdom of the locality. Farmers of both Greek and Roman times were aware of the value of manure and legumes, the need for drainage, and speculated on the optimum sowing rates. The decline of Rome meant that the knowledge of the Romans was neglected, although the manuscripts of Roman authors may have been preserved in monasteries. The role of the Romans as promoters of agricultural knowledge was taken over by the Arabs, who as a result of their remarkable expansion east to India and west to Spain acquired and transmitted new crops, and also produced, in the tenth century, manuals of agriculture partly based upon Greek writings. The great innovations of the early medieval period – the heavy plough, the three-field system, the horseshoe and horse-collar, were not dependent upon any scientific understanding. Nor did the spread and adoption of new crops such as turnip and clover from the fifteenth century onwards require more than observation to confirm their value to farmers. It was not until the seventeenth century that general advances began to be made in science; and only later in the eighteenth century that advances in chemistry and plant biology by Joseph Priestly, Antoine Lavoisier, Nicolas-Théodore de Saussure and Erasmus Darwin laid the basis for modern agricultural research.

The application of science to agriculture

From the middle of the nineteenth century there were concerted efforts to apply science to agriculture by the setting up of research institutions and experimental farms which would test old and new knowledge and practices. For the most part these institutions were financed by the state, for few farmers had the knowledge, time or resources to undertake long-term investigations; and because the results of most research became widely available, private enterprise was not interested. Nonetheless the earliest experimental farm in England, at Rothamsted in 1843, was financed privately by John Lawes. More important was the foundation of a state research institute at Mockern in Saxony in 1851. Inspired by the work of Albrecht Thaer and Justus von Liebig, Mockern prompted a remarkable expansion of research stations in Europe; by 1900 there were 500, and they employed over 1500 scientists. The example of Mockern stimulated a similar expansion in the United States; in

Table 9.1 Research and extension, 1965

	Research expenditure per farm, $US per year	Extension workers per 1000 farms
North America	93.1	2.2
Northern Europe	32.6	2.7
Eastern Europe and Russia	7.5	1.1
East Asia	7.2	2.0
Middle East and North Africa	4.9	2.3
Tropical Africa	2.8	1.9
Southern Europe	2.4	0.5
Latin America	1.6	0.3
South and South-East Asia	0.4	0.4

Source: R. E. Evenson and Y. Kislev, *Agricultural Research and Productivity*, New York, 1975, p. 16.

1862 the United States Department of Agriculture was founded, and in the same year each state made grants of land to found colleges which included agricultural departments. In 1887 the Hatch Act provided federal finance for agricultural research; the same year saw the first experimental farm in Canada, although the first research station was not established until 1906. In Australia the first agricultural research institute was not established until 1924. In England a number of independent research institutes, mainly in universities, were established in the late nineteenth century, but there was no state support for agricultural research until 1909 and funds increased very slowly until after the Second World War. In the twentieth century there has been a steady increase in research funded by industry; and in the United States research funded by the chemical industry has increased rapidly. Indeed, by the 1960s half the expenditure upon agricultural research in the United States was undertaken by the private sector. Agricultural research had by then spread throughout the world, although in terms of expenditure, it was still concentrated in North America and Northern Europe (table 9.1).

The transmission of knowledge to farmers

There is a great gulf between the work of experimental stations and the ordinary farmer; and in the past there was an equally large gulf between the practices of the best farmers and the majority. One way in which this gap has been bridged has been the book. Both Greek and Roman writers produced guides to farm management, but with the decline of Rome there was a long silence until the revival of science in the Arab world. Two manuals on agriculture were written in the early tenth century; but the most influential, the *Kitab al-fitaha* of Ibn al'Awwain, was written in the twelfth century, after the great age of Arab agriculture. By then Western Europe was awakening. Walter of Henley's *Husbandry* was written in the thirteenth century. But the invention of printing must have accelerated the diffusion of knowledge; Pietro de Crescenzi's manuscript of 1304 was, in 1574, the first agricultural work printed, and the sixteenth century saw a steady increase in the publication of agricultural works in most West European languages. The seventeenth century saw a widening interest in agriculture and allied activities, but it was in the eighteenth century that there was a great rise in published items upon agriculture, as the case of Denmark exemplifies (figure 9.1). In England Arthur Young published his first book in 1768, whilst during the Napoleonic Wars the Board of Agriculture promoted a considerable agricultural literature describing the agricultural practices of the time and advocating the adoption of the better methods. In the late seventeenth century the book began to be supplemented by the periodical. The number of agricultural periodicals published per year in England rose from an average of 0.3 in the 1680s to 7.5 in the 1790s, 30.8 in the 1840s and to over 100 in the 1890s. The great rise in the number of periodicals was partly a result of innovations in printing; the use of continuous rolls of paper in the 1790s, and the application of power to printing, quickened the process and lowered the cost. In the late eighteenth century the agricultural periodicals probably had a limited impact, but by the early Victorian period agricultural periodicals had a readership of 50–60,000. By the late 1930s four-fifths of British farmers regularly read articles on farming in the local press; about half read either the *Farmers' Weekly* or the *Farmer and Stockbreeder*. Thirty years later, 87 per cent read a farming

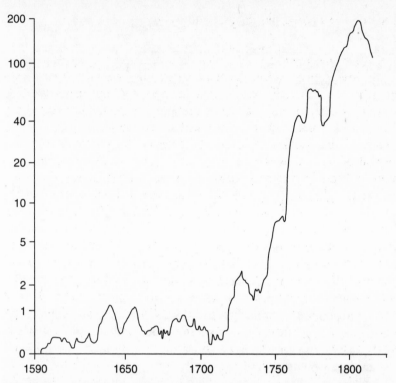

Figure 9.1 The annual production of agricultural treatises in Denmark and Schleswig-Holstein between 1590 and 1814: 10-year moving averages.
(*Source*: T. Kjaergaard, 'Origins of economic growth in European societies since the XVth century: the case of agriculture', *Journal of European Economic History*, 15, 1986, pp. 591–8.)

magazine, although only half had ever tried any of the innovations suggested in these periodicals.

Literacy

Although information on farming methods was available in printed books from the sixteenth century onwards, the number of these printed was small, and the circulation of information limited by the extent of literacy. The progress of literacy in Europe is not easy to trace. The inability to sign one's name in documents such as wills or marriage registers has been used to trace its rise, since there is

Table 9.2 Percentage illiterate by occupational groups, England,
1754–1844

	1754–1784	1785–1814	1815–1844
Gentry	0	1	3
Yeomen	19	18	17
Husbandmen	46	56	52
Labourers	59	65	66
All	36	39	35

Source: R. Schofield, 'Dimensions of illiteracy, 1750–1850', *Explorations in Economic History*, 10 (1973), 437–54.

some evidence that those who could sign their name could read and write. The ability to read and write varied greatly by occupation (table 9.2). In eighteenth- and nineteenth-century England virtually all the gentry – landowners – were literate, but amongst the yeomen – substantial farmers who did not let land out – nearly a fifth could not read in the first half of the nineteenth century. Among husbandmen, the great majority of farmers, only half were literate, and amongst labourers only one-third.

International comparisons of the progress of literacy are probably hazardous, but England, Scotland, and particularly New England, had a higher rate of literacy than other parts of European settlement in the seventeenth century. The figures in table 9.3 refer to estimates for the total population; urban literacy was higher than rural. By the middle of the seventeenth century probably a third of the rural population of England and New England were literate, enough, probably, for new ideas to spread to the leaders of rural society and then spread by exhortation or emulation amongst the illiterate. In France in 1800 over half the rural population were still illiterate, but there was a substantial regional difference; literacy was far greater in the north than the south.

Agricultural societies and extension officers

Farmers learned a lot from each other; this was partly achieved simply by observing their neighbours' fields, but from the eight-

Table 9.3 Percentage unable to sign their name (males)

	c.1500	c.1550	c.1640	c.1715	c.1750	c.1800	c.1890	c.1911
England	90	89	70	55	40	38	30	1
France	–	–	–	70[a]	–	53[b]	–	–
Belgium	–	–	–	–	–	39[c]	–	–
Scotland	–	–	–	67[d]	–	10	–	–
East Prussia	–	–	–	–	90	60	–	–
New England	–	–	39[e]	31[f]	16[g]	–	–	–

[a] 1686–90.
[b] 1786–90.
[c] Late eighteenth century.
[d] 1675.
[e] 1660.
[f] 1710.
[g] 1760.

Source: D. Cressy, *Literacy and the Social Order: Reading and Writing in Tudor and Stuart England*, Cambridge, 1980, pp. 176, 177, 178.

eenth century they began to form societies or clubs; these might be political or social in purpose, or aimed at promoting new ideas. Some of the societies were the preserve of landlords, but increasingly they encompassed a fair proportion of ordinary farmers. They appeared in France and Italy in the 1750s; a society for the advancement of agriculture was founded in the Netherlands in 1776; and the first major society in England, the Bath and West, the following year. Farmers' associations, based upon smaller districts than the societies, appeared in Faversham in 1727 and Brecon in 1777; by 1807 there was 25 in England, by the 1870s there were 600. There was an equally rapid growth in the United States; by 1860 there were 900 farmers' associations. The larger societies had annual shows – in the United States fairs – that displayed new equipment, judged livestock and encouraged good practices, such as ploughing, by prize competitions.

It would seem that by the nineteenth century the degree of literacy and the spread of farmers' associations would have been sufficient channels to spread new knowledge and practices to farmers. But at the end of the nineteenth century many farms in Europe and North America were still remarkably backward. There thus arose a new link in the chain of knowledge, the extension or advisory officer, whose aim was to advise farmers and in particular to promote innovations.

In England the Advisory Service began in 1912, although it had no more than a handful of officers until after the Second World War. In the United States federal funds for advisory work began in 1914, but in the 1930s soil erosion in the Great Plains prompted the appointment of advisory officers to promote conservation methods. In Denmark the government had begun an embryonic service much earlier, in the 1880s, when advisers on livestock and plant breeding were financed with state funds.

Extension work spread slowly in much of Europe, particularly in the south; none the less in Italy the attempt to increase wheat yields in the 1920s – Mussolini's 'Battle for Bread' – prompted the establishment of 25,000 demonstration sites for new wheat varieties. But the expansion of advisory services has come largely since the end of the Second World War, although there was still a marked difference between the provision of officers between northern and southern Europe in the 1950s (table 9.4).

Table 9.4 Number of farms over 1 hectare per extension officer, 1953

Netherlands	190	Switzerland	720
England and Wales	240	Austria	730
Scotland	260	Greece	900
Norway	410	France	1600
Germany	440	Italy	2700
Sweden	500	Portugal	6500
Belgium	510		

Source: P. Lamartine Yates, *Food, Land and Manpower in Western Europe*, London, 1960, p. 203.

The process of diffusion

The means by which either innovations or best practices can be communicated to farmers rapidly increased in the nineteenth century, as did their knowledge, and so too did the rate of adoption of new techniques. As mentioned above, modern studies of the rate of adoption have shown that early adopters are few, and are generally better educated, possess larger farms than average and are often young. In Britain much research has emphasized the role of landlords in experimenting with new crops or methods on their home farms, and encouraging their tenants to adopt them. In the eighteenth century great landlords were prominent in introducing turnips and clover and encouraging the improvement of livestock. It may be that early historians exaggerated the role of Charles Townshend and Thomas Coke of Holkham; they certainly underestimated the new class of men, the stewards and land agents, who undertook most of the day-to-day running of estates. In Scotland much of the improvement of agriculture in the second half of the eighteenth century was due to the activities of the landlords who acquired the Annexed estates forfeit to the Crown after the rising of 1745. Many of these new landlords were linked by blood or marriage, and corresponded regularly with each other upon agricultural matters. Essential to estate improvement was the land surveyor, who charted the estate and its boundaries, advised upon new buildings and practices, and set rents. The surveyors' work

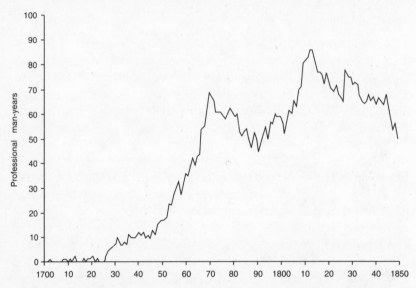

Figure 9.2　The contribution of land surveyors to estate improvement in Scotland, 1700–1850. (*Source*: I. H. Adams, 'The agents of agricultural change', in M. L. Parry and T. R. Slater (eds), *The Making of the Scottish Countryside*, London, 1980, p. 167.)

(figure 9.2) demonstrates the sharp rate of improvement in Scottish farming in the second half of the eighteenth century.

Landlords also lead the way in innovation elsewhere in Europe, notably in Prussia after the reforms of 1807 led to the formation of large estates run, not by tenant farmers, but by the owner. Albrecht Thaer's work on agriculture, which promolgated English farming methods, was influential in the great improvements to farming that took place after the end of the Napoleonic Wars. In contrast, historians have argued that French landlords were far less active, acting as little more than *rentiers*, investing little in improvement and all too often being absentee owners.

But it was not only landlords who acted as agents of change: amongst farmers it was the occupiers of large farms who were the first to adopt new techniques. In the case of the adoption of machinery this was almost inevitable, for a large acreage was necessary if machines like the reaper or the combine harvester were to be profitable. Thus in New York State in 1850 the early adopters of the reaper not only possessed larger than average farms but were often professional men with a non-farm income, and thus prepared to take risks.

For the farmer with a small holding – the great majority of West European farmers – risk avoidance was perhaps a stronger motive than the prospect of profit that innovations brought. Certainly the spread of innovations before the nineteenth century was remarkably slow. This may be because innovations spread from the first farms to adopt solely by emulation, so that the innovation spread across the countryside like a ripple in a pond when a stone is dropped. The rate of diffusion was remarkably slow. One historian has calculated that the domestication of plants and the beginnings of agriculture – which first appeared in the Middle East in about 8000 BC – took 2800 years to reach Northern Europe, a rate of spread of approximately one mile a year. In the 1790s Coke of Holkham, who held annual sheep-shearings, partly to promote his ideas, gloomily estimated that his advice travelled at no more than a mile a year. Certainly there was always a long lag between an innovation and its complete adoption. Thus the horse replaced the ox on some farms in the Paris basin in the twelfth century, but did not finally usurp the ox on a majority of farms in Western Europe until the nineteenth century. The progress of innovations in England shows how slow the rate of adoption was and how it has accelerated in the twentieth century (figure 9.3). The turnip was first grown as a field crop in the middle of the seventeenth century; it had been introduced to nearly every region by the middle of the eighteenth century, but it occupied only about 8 per cent of the country's arable in 1801 and did not reach the maximum of nearly one-fifth until the 1850s and 1860s. The seed drill exemplifies some of the problems of diffusion. Jethro Tull built a seed drill, but had difficulties in getting his workers to use it; and certainly his and other early drills were not efficient. It was not until the 1780s that a efficient drill was designed, by James Cooke; yet at the end of the Napoleonic Wars it was rare outside East Anglia or the north-east of England, and not until the 1850s was it commonplace. After 1850 the rate of adoption picked up. The first reapers were used in the 1850s, and by 1900 80 per cent of British grain was cut by the reaper-binder; the first combine harvester in England dates from 1927, but by the 1970s the reaper-binder was confined to farms with small acreages, small fields and steep slopes. In the post-war period the rate of adoption has dramatically increased, so that the

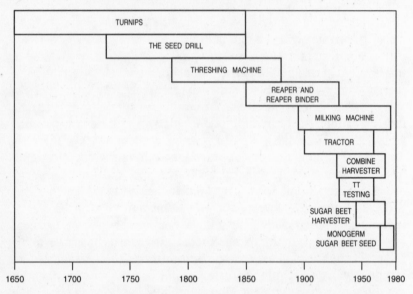

Figure 9.3 The chronology of innovation. The bar represents the time between the first use of an innovation and its full adoption.

sugar beet harvester, the potato harvester, monogerm sugar beet seed and a host of other innovations all supplanted earlier practices in less than two decades (figure 9.3).

The state and the farmer

The role of the state in the improvement of agriculture has often been neglected. Yet much of the progress of agriculture has been accelerated since the formation of strong centralized states in the sixteenth century. Securing internal peace has been an obvious advantage of the nation-state; the Thirty Years War had effects upon German population and agriculture like those of the wars in Vietnam and Cambodia in the 1960s or in parts of Africa in the 1970s. The establishment of a legal system regulated inheritance and the conveyancing of land. In the eighteenth century and later it required national legislation to free the serf, pass Enclosure Acts, and, in the twentieth century, to promote the consolidation of fragmented holdings. Less obvious advantages were the institution of a common system of weights and measures. The metric system was introduced by Napoleon; the British imperial system was not adopted until the early nineteenth century, and with slight modifications prevailed in the English-speaking countries until recently. The state has had to intervene in numerous other ways. For example, the spread of cattle disease has had disastrous consequences for farmers; its control or partial control had to await the availability of antibiotics and vaccines after 1945. Before then quarantine, the control of internal movements of animals, and compensation for animals compulsorily destroyed all required central legislation; such legislation was passed in England as early as 1714. The slow move to protect the consumer has also, in the long run, benefited the farmer. In the nineteenth century milk was both adulterated and often infectious. It required legislation to improve hygiene, prevent adulteration and make milk a satisfactory product; legislation has also regulated the quality of the products that farmers buy, such as seeds and fertilizers.

This chapter has already shown the role that governments have taken in the undertaking and transmission of scientific advance in agriculture. Equally significant has been the role of the state in protecting farmers from imports and subsidizing improvements. This is not new and has been of major importance over the last two hundred years. Nearly all European nation-states protected their farmers by tariffs upon imported grain prior to the nineteenth century. There were two reasons for this. In the first place most governments believed that the provision of an adequate food supply was a prime aim, not least in the time of war. Secondly, most European governments were formed from the landowning classes who wished to protect their own incomes. In Britain tariffs on the import of grain and other agricultural products existed until the conversion to free trade and the repeal of the Corn Laws in 1846. Until the emergence of much cheaper producers in North America and Australia, and above all the introduction of refrigeration, which removed the protection that perishability provided, other European countries also moved towards free trade. In the 1880s, however, imports of grain, meat, butter and cheese undercut most European farmers and with few exceptions tariffs were introduced. France raised its tariffs in the 1880s, as did Germany, Italy, Switzerland, Sweden, Spain and Portugal. Only in Britain, Denmark and the Netherlands did free trade prevail, and in all three countries the trend was to livestock production, using cheap imported grain.

These tariffs did not end the importation of overseas foods in Europe. Britain became largely dependent upon imported food, and even in Germany where tariffs had been imposed, an increased proportion of food came from abroad by 1914. The First World War was a sharp reminder to all European countries of the need for food security. Yet immediately after the end of the war, there was a reversion to free trade; however, this did not last long. Tariffs were reintroduced, and even Britain began to protect its farmers by the introduction of tariffs, quotas, and subsidies for improvements such as liming. In the United States, over-production in the 1930s prompted government to pay farmers not to grow certain crops.

It was during this period that economists pointed to the almost universal difference between agricultural and non-agricultural incomes in Western countries, and some argued that government support was necessary to achieve parity of incomes. The Second World War persuaded many post-war politicians of the need to have a secure home supply of food, and the shortages of the period between 1945 and 1951 led most countries to subsidize land reclamation and other improvements; there was also in the 1950s a reversion to tariff protection, although Britain and Denmark continued to allow relatively free access to overseas producers. Thus the Common Agricultural Policy of the EEC, which since 1968 has protected farmers from the competition of overseas producers, was not a new policy.

The role of government support for agriculture in Western Europe – and in different ways in North America – can hardly be underestimated. In Britain, both under the system of guaranteed prices and subsidies that prevailed before entry to the EEC in 1973, and under the Common Agricultural Policy since then, net farm income has often been equivalent to the government support the national farm receives. In short, it can be doubted if the prodigious advance in technical efficiency would have been achieved without government support.

Conclusions

There is no doubt that the means by which knowledge of new techniques was transmitted to farmers greatly improved in the nineteenth century and have accelerated since. Before the mid-nineteenth century it must be doubted if scientific advance had much effect upon agriculture. Since then it has been prodigious, with Louis Pasteur's work on the transmission of disease leading to its control among plants and animals, and Gregor Mendel's work on peas leading to modern plant breeding.

Conclusions

Over the last two hundred years the most striking feature of the world's economic change has been the remarkable growth of manufacturing and service industries. It has been estimated that world industrial output increased nearly ninetyfold between 1750 and 1980, and industrial output *per capita* of the total population in 1980 was fifteen times what it was in 1750. In comparison, agricultural growth has been modest, output having risen at most twentyfold, and productivity perhaps three times. The role of agriculture in the world and national economies is consequently greatly diminished. Two centuries ago, agriculture employed three-quarters of the population of Western Europe, and produced about one-half of the income; these figures are now much lower, and indeed in many countries agriculture accounts for less than 5 per cent of employment or income.

None the less the modernization of agriculture has made a great contribution to the economic progress of the Western world. First and foremost, the problems of famine and hunger have been overcome. In the eighteenth century most European nations had a meagre food supply, averaging 2000 calories *per caput* per day, roughly comparable with tropical Africa at present and well below the current food supplies of Latin America and most Asian nations. Although the rich ate well, most of the poor, the majority of the population, did not. Low food supplies were a result of very low agricultural productivity and poverty. Because much of the population was chronically undernourished, any shortfall in harvest, whether due to flood, drought or crop disease, led to famines and a rise in the death rate. Western Europe began to overcome the problem of famine in the seventeenth century. The last famine in England was in the 1620s, in Scotland in the 1690s, in Germany in 1732 and in France in 1795. The last great famine, in which a million died out of a population of 8 million, was in Ireland between 1845 and 1851.

The elimination of famine was partly due to an increase in agricultural productivity, but also to better transport and improved organization of relief. By the middle of the nineteenth century, most countries in the West had a national food supply, from domestic production and imports, capable of providing an adequate diet. But malnutrition still persisted and the slow reduction was due not only to the increase in food supplies but to the slow improvement of incomes. As people, even the poorest, improved their income, so the symptoms of malnutrition disappeared, although the League of Nations still regarded poor nutrition as a major problem in Europe in the 1920s and 1930s. In the long run an ever more efficient agricultural system has produced food whose real cost has been falling; in the nineteenth century most of the population of Western Europe spent 70 per cent or more of their income upon food; this has now fallen to 20 per cent or less. The provision of more food, and generally a better diet – although this latter point is now debatable – has had other beneficial effects. Although the causes of the great fall in the death rate are still a matter of controversy, it is likely that improved nutrition made an important contribution, for malnutrition impaired the body's immune system, and reduced the ability to resist infectious disease. Indeed malnutrition, in a synergetic relationship with infectious disease, still accounts for a high proportion of deaths, particularly infant and child deaths, in the developing countries today.

The provision of a better diet has not been farming's only contribution to the greater prosperity that modern economic growth has brought. Many historians believe that industrialization could not have got under way without a major contribution from the agricultural sector, which until the eighteenth century dominated employment, wealth and political power. Thus an increase in agricultural productivity allowed a surplus above the needs of the agricultural populations to feed an urban industrial population; furthermore it provided a cheaper food supply, which in the early stages of the industrial revolution allowed low wages and the accumulation of capital for further investment in industry. In many countries, agriculture also provided the labour force for the new industries. Death rates in most towns before the mid-nineteenth century were above those in rural areas, and indeed above birth rates in the towns. As a result the growth of an industrial labour force was dependent upon rural–urban migration. At first much of this migration may have been of those underemployed in the countryside, but migration was sustained later only by a growth in agricultural productivity.

The early industrial revolution was dependent upon agriculture for much of its raw materials. The first factory industries were textiles, and in Europe wool and in the United States cotton were needed. But agriculture also supplied hides, flax, dyes and other important raw materials. Only later in the process of economic development, when engineering became the leading sector, did inorganic raw materials become dominant.

The factories of the new society needed, of course, a market for factory-made goods. In the early stages of industrialization the rural population made up a considerable part of the market, and farms have been estimated to have taken one-third of Britain's iron production in the eighteenth century. An effective demand for industrial goods required a prosperous agricultural population, only possible if productivity growth was taking place in agriculture. This does not exhaust the contributions agriculture made to the early stages of economic growth. Industry needed investment, and the landowners were an important source of capital, whilst at a national level exports of agricultural products were an important source of income for investment in industry. In early eighteenth-century England, cereals were an important export, although exports were of most importance in the early development of Australia, Canada, New Zealand and the United States. Even at the beginning of this century, when the United States had become the leading industrial nation, much of her exports were agricultural.

Until the mid-nineteenth century agriculture made important contributions to industrialization, but then the flow, as it were, began to reverse. From then onwards agriculture began to become dependent upon industry for its inputs. At first this had a limited impact upon agricultural productivity, but slowly, and particularly after the decline of the agricultural labour force, productivity began to increase, culminating in the remarkable technical achievements of the last half century. But over the last twenty or thirty years, there has been a fall from grace; farmers have lost the goodwill of the urban population, and have become as well a major economic problem.

The causes of this go back to at least the inter-war period. In the 1920s and 1930s many economists and politicians pointed out that agricultural incomes were well below non-agricultural incomes; it was also noted that agricultural producers were subject to greater fluctuations in price than most industrial products, due to the dependence of harvest upon weather and plant disease. Thus politicians slowly tried first to stabilize prices and secondly to help farmers achieve parity with industrial incomes. Hence in the 1920s and 1930s tariffs to protect home farmers, schemes in the United States to pay farmers not go grow crops in surplus, and subsidies to aid farmers to improve their land all became common. During the Second World War, and indeed down to the early 1950s, there was a acute world shortage of food, and farmers were encouraged to produce almost regardless of cost. However, by the 1950s the disruption of the war was over and world food supplies were back to normal.

Three critical forces developed in the 1950s. First, most Western countries were committed to the protection – in some form or the other – of their farmers and paid lip service to the idea of parity. The discipline of the market was slowly eroded. Second the technical advances in fertilizers, pesticides and new varieties were giving unprecedented increases in output. Third, the rate of increase in demand was slowing. This was due partly to the comparatively slow rate of population growth in the post-war period, but more importantly to the greater affluence of the populations of the Western world. Except for the poorest, incomes were sufficient to obtain a more than adequate diet which included not only the staples of bread and potatoes, but large quantities of livestock products, fruit and vegetables. Any increases in income did not lead to proportional increases in food consumption. Thus the supply of foodstuffs exceeded demand. Over the last twenty years, output in the EEC has risen at an average of 2 per cent per annum, but demand by only 0.5 per cent. By the late 1970s surpluses were appearing in the United States and the EEC and the cost of protection, subsidy and storage was becoming politically untenable. In the 1980s the efforts of the EEC and the United States to export their surplus grain was leading to the prospect of trade wars and having disastrous effects upon the economies of many other countries, such as Australia. At the same time the farmers, the apparent beneficiaries of technological advance and protection, were not prospering; in the 1970s and 1980s real incomes fell and in the 1980s bankruptcies became widespread.

To complete the farmer's woes, he had lost the goodwill of the public for quite different reasons. The adoption of machinery and chemicals have had very adverse effects. The excessive use of nitrates has polluted groundwater in parts of the United States and Britain; pesticides have poisoned birds, herbicides have destroyed much of the flora of the countryside. Fields have been enlarged and hedgerows removed, so destroying the habitat of birds and small mammals and changing for the worse the appearance of the countryside.

Thus the triumphant advance of agriculture as a productive force has turned sour in the 1980s, for the agricultural population itself, and for the consumer, as food scare follows food scare. This is sad, for the farming community has served the nations well over the last two centuries.

Further Reading

Abel, W., *Agricultural Fluctuations in Western Europe from the Thirteenth to the Twentieth Centuries*, London, 1980.

Allen, R. C., 'The growth of labour productivity in early modern English agriculture', *Explorations in Economic History*, 25 (1988), 117–46.

Anderson, B. L. and A. J. Latham, *The Market in History*, London, 1986.

Andrews, D., M. Mitchell and A. Weber, *The Development of Agriculture in Germany and the UK: Comparative Time Series, 1870–1975*. Wye College, Ashford, Kent, 1979.

Appleby, J., 'Commercial farming and the agrarian myth in the Early Republic', *Journal of American History*, 68 (1982), 833–49.

Atack, J. and F. Bateman, 'Self-sufficiency and the marketable surplus in the rural north, 1860', *Agricultural History*, 58 (1984), 296–313.

Bairoch, P., 'Agriculture and the industrial revolution', in C. Cipolla (ed.), *The Fontana Economic History of Europe*, vol. 3, *The Industrial Revolution*, London, 1980.

Bicanic, R., *Turning Points in Economic Development*, The Hague, 1972.

Biddick, K., 'Medieval English peasants and market involvement', *Journal of Economic History*, 45 (1985), 823–31.

Blum, J., *The End of the Old Order in Europe*, Princeton, 1978.

Bogue, A., 'Changes in mechanical and plant technology: the Corn Belt 1910–1940', *Journal of Economic History*, 43 (1983), 1–21.

Bowers, J., 'The economics of agribusiness', in M. J. Healey and B. W. Ilbery (eds), *The Industrialization of the Countryside*, Norwich, 1985, pp. 29–44.

Bowler, I., 'Some consequences of the industrialization of agriculture in the European community', in M. J. Healey and B. W. Ilbery (eds), *The Industrialization of the Countryside*, Norwich, 1985, pp. 75–98.

Britnell, R. H., 'The proliferation of markets in England 1200–1349', *Economic History Review*, 34 (1981), 209–21.

Burns, J. A., 'The UK food chain with particular reference to the interrelations between manufacturers and distribution', *Journal of Agricultural Economics*, 34 (1983), 361–78.

Butlin, R., 'The enclosure of open fields and extinction of common rights in England, circa 1600–1750: a review', in H. S. Fox and R. Butlin (eds), *Change in the Countryside: Essays on Rural England 1500–1900*, London, 1979, pp. 65–82.

Chorley, G., 'The agricultural revolution in Northern Europe, 1750–1880', *Economic History Review*, 34 (1981), 71–93.

Collins, E. J. T., 'Labour supply and demand in European agriculture 1800–1880', in E. L. Jones and S. J. Woolf (eds), *Agrarian Change and Economic Development: The Historical Problems*, London, 1969, pp. 61–94.

Collins, E. J. T., 'The diffusion of the threshing machine in Britain, 1790–1880', *Tools and Tillage*, 2 (1972), 16–33.

Dodgshon, R. A., *The European Past, Social Evolution and Spatial Order*, Basingstoke, 1987.

Dovring, F., 'The share of agriculture in a growing population', *Monthly Bulletin of Agricultural Economics and Statistics*, 8 (1959), 1–11.

Dovring, F., *Land and Labour in Europe in the Twentieth Century*, The Hague, 1965.

Dovring, F., 'The transformation of European agriculture', in H. Habakkuk and M. Postan (eds), *The Cambridge Economic History of Europe*, vol. 6: *The Industrial Revolutions and After*, Cambridge, 1965, pp. 604–67.

Dunsdorf, E., *The Australian Wheat Growing Industry, 1788–1948*. Melbourne, 1956.

Fisher, F. J., 'The development of the London food market 1540–1640', *Economic History Review*, 5 (1934–5), 46–64.

Fite, G. C., *The Farmers' Frontier 1865–1900*, New York, 1966.

Food and Agriculture Organization, *Agricultural Adjustment in Developed Countries*, Rome, 1972.

Forster, R., 'Obstacles to agricultural growth in eighteenth-century France', *American Historical Review*, 75 (1970), 1600–15.

Fox, H. S., 'Local farmers' associations and the circulation of agricultural information in nineteenth-century England', in H. S. Fox and R. A. Butlin (eds), *Change in the Countryside: Essays on Rural England 1500–1900*, London, 1979, pp. 43–64.

Franklin, S. H., *The European Peasantry: The Final Phase*, London, 1969.

Gates, P. W., *The Farmers' Age: Agriculture 1815–1860*, New York, 1960.

Goddard, N., 'Agricultural literature', in G. E. Mingay (ed.), *The Agrarian History of England and Wales*, vol. 6: *1750–1850*, Cambridge, 1989, pp. 365–78.

Goodman, D., B. Sorj and J. Wilkinson, *From Farming to Biotechnology: A Theory of Agro-industrial Development*, Oxford, 1987.

Grantham, G., 'The diffusion of the New Husbandry in northern France, 1815–1840', *Journal of Economic History*, 38 (1978), 311–37.

Grantham, G., 'The persistence of open field farming in nineteenth century France', *Journal of Economic History*, 40 (1980), 515–31.

Grigg, D., 'The world's agricultural labour force 1800–1970', *Geography*, 60 (1975), 194–202.

Grigg, D., *Population Growth and Agrarian Change: An Historical Perspective*, Cambridge, 1980.

Grigg, D., *The Dynamics of Agricultural Change: The Historical Experience*, London, 1982.

Grigg, D., 'Farm size in England and Wales', *Agricultural History Review*, 35 (1987), 179–89.

Grigg, D., *English Agriculture: An Historical Perspective*, Oxford, 1989.

Hayami, Y. and V. W. Ruttan, *Agricultural Development: An International Perspective*, Baltimore, 1971.

Heywood, C., 'The role of the peasantry in French industrialisation 1815–30', *Economic History Review*, 34 (1980), 359–76.

Hohenburg, P., 'Maize in French agriculture', *Journal of European Economic History*, 6 (1977), 63–102.

International Labour Office, *Why Labour Leaves the Land*, Geneva, 1960.

Johnston, B. F. and P. Kilby, *Agriculture and Structural Transformation*, Oxford, 1975.

Johnston, B. F. and S. T. Nielsen, 'Agricultural and structural transformation in a developing economy', *Economic Development and Cultural Change*, 14 (1966), 279–301.

Jones, E. L. 'The agricultural labour market in England 1793–1872', *Economic History Review*, 17 (1964–5), 322–38.

Jones, E. L., *The European Miracle: Environments, Economics and Geopolitics in the History of Europe and Asia*, Cambridge, 1987.

Jones, G. E., 'The diffusion of agricultural innovations', in I. Burton and P. W. Kates (eds), *Readings in Resource Management and Conservation*, Chicago, 1965, pp. 475–92.

Kerridge, E., 'The agricultural revolution reconsidered', *Agricultural History*, 43 (1969), 464–74.

Kreidte, P., *Peasants, Landlords and Merchant Capitalists: Europe and the World Economy 1500–1800*, Leamington Spa, 1983.

Ladurie, E. LeRoy and J. Goy, *Tithe and Agrarian History from the Fourteenth to Nineteenth Centuries*, Cambridge, 1982.

Mayhew, A., 'Structural reform and the future of West German agriculture', *Geographical Review*, 60 (1970), 54–68.

Mingay, G. E., 'The agricultural revolution in English history: a reconsideration', *Agricultural history*, 43 (1969), 123–33.

Newell, W. H., 'The agricultural revolution in nineteenth century France', *Journal of Economic History*, 33 (1973), 697–731.

North, D. C., 'Oceanic freight rates and economic development 1750–1913', *Journal of Economic History*, 18 (1958), 537–56.

North, D. C., 'Sources of productivity change in oceanic shipping 1600–1850', *Journal of Political Economy*, 76 (1968), 953–70.

O'Brien, P. K., 'Transport and economic growth in Western Europe 1830–1914', *Journal of European Economic History*, 11 (1982), 335–67.

O'Brien, P. K., D. Heath and C. Keyder, 'Agricultural efficiency in Britain and France 1815–1914', *Journal of European Economic History*, 6 (1977), 339–91.

OECD (Office for Economic Co-operation and Development), *Problems of Manpower in Agriculture*, Paris, 1964.

OECD, *Agriculture and Economic Growth*, Paris, 1965.

Ojala, E. M., *Agriculture and Economic Progress*, London, 1952.

Parry, J. H., 'Transport and trade routes', in C. H. Wilson and E. E. Rich (eds), *The Cambridge Economic History of Europe*, vol. 5: *The Economic Organization of Early Modern Europe*, Cambridge, 1967.

Peet, J. R., 'The spatial expansion of commercial agriculture in the nineteenth century; a von Thunen interpretation', *Economic Geography*, 45 (1969), 283–301.

Perkins, J. A., 'The agricultural revolution in Germany 1850–1914', *Journal of European Economic History*, 10 (1981), 71–118.

Pounds, N. J. G., *An Historical Geography of Europe 1800–1914*, Cambridge, 1985.

Pred, A., *Place, Practice and Structure*, Cambridge, 1986.

Price, R., 'The onset of labour shortage in nineteenth century French agriculture', *Economic History Review*, 28 (1975), 260–77.

Rasmussen, W. D., 'The impact of technological change in American agriculture, 1862–1962', *Journal of Economic History*, 22 (1962), 578–91.

Rasmussen, W. D., 'The mechanization of agriculture', *Scientific American*, 247 (1982), 49–61.

Rothenberg, W. B., 'The market and Massachusetts farmers 1750–1855', *Journal of Economic History*, 41 (1981), 283–314.

Schlebecker, J. T., *Whereby We Thrive: A History of American Farming 1607–1972*, Ames, Iowa, 1975.

Schultz, T. W., 'Evidence on farmer responses to economic opportunities from the early agrarian history of Western Europe', in C. Wharton, *Subsistence Agriculture and Economic Development*, London, 1970, pp. 105–10.

Shannon, F. A., *The Farmers' Last Frontier: Agriculture 1860–1897*, New York, 1963.

Simantov, A., 'The dynamics of growth and agriculture', *Zeitschrift für national ökonimie*, 27 (1967), 328–51.

Slicher van Bath, B. H., *The Agrarian History of Western Europe AD 500–1850*, London, 1963.

Slicher van Bath, B. H., 'Agriculture in the vital revolution', in E. E. Rich and C. H. Wilson (eds), *The Cambridge Economic History of Europe*: vol. 5: *The Economic Organization of Early Modern Europe*, Cambridge, 1977.

Staatz, J. M. and C. K. Eicher, 'Agricultural development ideas in historical perspective', in C. Eicher and J. Staatz (eds), *Agricultural Development in the Third World*, Baltimore, 1984, pp. 3–30.

Thienne, G., 'Agricultural change and its impact in rural areas', in T. Wild (ed.), *Urban and Rural Change in West Germany*, London, 1983.

Thompson, F. M. L., 'The Second Agricultural Revolution 1815–1880', *Economic History Review*, 21 (1968–9), 62–77.

Tracy, M., *Agriculture in Western Europe: Challenge and Response 1880–1980*, London, 1982.

Troughton, M., 'Process and response in the industrialization of agriculture', in G. Enyedi and I. Volgyes (eds), *The Effect of Modern Agriculture on Rural Development*, Oxford, 1982, pp. 213–28.

Wallace, I., 'Toward a geography of agribusiness', *Progress in Human Geography*, 9 (1985), 491–514.

Wallace, I. and W. Smith, 'Agribusiness in North America', in M. J. Healey and B. W. Ilbery (eds), *The Industrialization of the Countryside*, Norwich, 1985, pp. 57–74.

Wallerstein, I., *The Modern World-System. 1 Capitalist Agriculture and the Origins of the European World-Economy in the Sixteenth Century*, New York, 1974.

Warriner, D., *Economics of Peasant Farming*, London, 1964.

Wharton, C., *Subsistence Agriculture and Economic Development*, London, 1970.

White, L. T., *Medieval Technology and Social Change*, Ottawa, 1962.

Williams, D. B., *Agriculture in the Australian Economy*, London, 1982.

Yates, P. Lamartine, *Food Production in Western Europe*, London, 1940.

Yates, P. Lamartine, *Food, Land and Manpower in Western Europe*, London, 1960.

Youngson, A. J., 'The opening up of new territories', in H. J. Habakkuk and M. Postan (eds), *The Cambridge Economic History of Europe*, vol. 6: *The Industrial Revolutions and After: Incomes, Population and Technological Change*, Cambridge, 1965, pp. 139–211.

Index